A Physician's Witness to the Power of Shared Prayer

D0861700

A Physician's Witness to the Power of Shared Prayer

*William F. Haynes, Jr.,
M.D., F.A.C.C.*

Foreword by the
Very Reverend
James C. Fenhagen, Dean of the
General Theological Seminary

A Campion Book

Loyola University Press
Chicago

Printed in the United States of America

Loyola University Press
3441 North Ashland Avenue
Chicago, Illinois 60657

All scripture passages are taken from
the HOLY BIBLE, NEW INTERNATIONAL VERSION
© 1973, 1978 by the International Bible Society. Used
by permission.

The verse from Hymn 636 on page 28 is taken from
The Hymnal 1982. © Church Pension Fund

Library of Congress Cataloging-in-Publication Data
Haynes, William F.
      A physician's witness to the power of shared prayer/
   William F. Haynes, Jr. ; foreword by James Fenhagen.
         p.   cm.
      Includes bibliographical references.
      ISBN 0-8294-0697-2 (acid-free)
      1.   Prayer.   2.   Spiritual healing.   3.   Spiritual life.
   4.   Consolation.   5.   Haynes, William F.   I.   Title.
   BV220.H37   1990
   234'.13—dc20   90-47435
                                                      CIP

Contents

Foreword

Although I believe deeply that the Holy Spirit works in the world both individually and corporately to transform human life, I am not a "charismatic Christian," as the term is generally used in church circles today. I was, therefore, cautious when William Haynes asked me to write a foreword to *A Physician's Witness to the Power of Shared Prayer*, especially when I read of his experience with the Catholic Charismatic Conference and the Assemblies of God. It seemed, at first glance, that our particular pilgrimages had taken us on very different, and not always compatible routes. What I discovered, however, as I read his book further, was that our paths were not as divergent as I had first thought and that the life in Christ which we both share made it possible to move beyond innate cautiousness to connection. Although we have talked on the phone, Dr. Haynes and I have never met. He knew of my interest in the life of prayer, and we had friends in common. It was on this basis that I agreed to read his manuscript and eventually to write this foreword. I have been deeply rewarded by the opportunity given to me to share in William Haynes very moving and very powerful witness.

A Physician's Witness addresses three concerns that are especially important when we speak of life of prayer in relation to the healing power of God. The first concern, which permeates the entire book, has to do with our ability to affirm without question the utter reliability of God's power and desire to heal. "Therefore, I tell you, " Jesus says to his disciples, "whatever you ask in prayer, believe that you have received it, and it will be yours" (Mark 11.24). Haynes tells how he learned to pray "affirmation prayers" and to write "love letters to God" from his mother. These prayers and letters became for him ways of affirming the truth of Jesus' promise, while at the same time acknowledging that God's response to our prayer for healing is never in our terms alone. But without the faith to affirm God's healing promise, our capacity as healer is severely limited. The numerous case studies of patients where healing came in so many different ways only makes sense in the context of this basic affirmation of faith. If we are to share in Jesus' healing ministry, we must believe that God does, indeed, heal.

William Haynes struggles throughout the book to walk the narrow path between religious piety and spiritual realism. Haynes expresses his concern that he "does not want to be thought of as an overly pious physician" and seeks to balance his desire to pray with his patients and bear witness to his faith by a deep commitment to the process of discernment. This second concern is important when sharing our faith with others and I very much appreciate Dr. Haynes's sensitivity to the uniqueness of other people's journeys—a uniqueness sometimes unknown even to them. It is this struggle to find a sense of balance that makes William Haynes's witness both powerful and authentic.

The third concern that Haynes addresses that I find particularly helpful has to do with the need for the helper to find help for him or herself. Haynes speaks wisely of how stress contributes to illness and offers helpful suggestions toward developing the kind of Christ-centered life that makes it possible for us to care for others. "In order to be contemplative," Haynes writes, "I must have an unusual reconciliation and unity with God, a constant communication with God, a feeling that he is part of me and I a part of him and the rest of his creation. This communication and contemplation create a unity—a bonding of myself, God, and his world. The result is love in action" (page 88). This, I believe, is as good a statement of healthy Christian spirituality as I have read anywhere, and it undergirds all the practical suggestions that Haynes offers to all and everyone ready to say yes to the invitation offered to us by the Spirit.

William Haynes's book is a small book that is both wise and simple. It is an honest witness of a thoughtful cardiologist who has learned to care for his patients in a new way, and discovered through the power of the Holy Spirit, a new way to care for himself.

The Very Reverend James C. Fenhagen
Dean of the General Theological Seminary

Preface

This book is meant to help those who have heartaches, are wounded and discouraged, and are carrying heavy burdens. Though it cannot speak to all of life's low points, nevertheless, it is a book of hope and encouragement. The power of prayer will be illustrated not only in my own situation but in those of a number of patients. It is a book to build our faith.

Although written from a physician's perspective, the book is intended to serve as a practical guide for not only those in the various medical fields but also for clergy, prayer groups, and laypeople interested in the interaction of illness with the healing power of prayer.

This is a true story of my own brokenness, transformation, and enhanced awareness of God's presence in my personal life and professional life as well. This book describes my journey on the road I have been traveling since early childhood, which led to a very steep climb (crisis) in mid-adulthood, and which I still travel today. As scripture says,

> I have told you these things, so that in me you may have peace. In this world you will have trouble. But take heart! I have overcome the world.

> John 16.33

Acknowledgments

My heartfelt thanks go to Sr. Miriam Murphy, Ph.D., for her encouragement in writing this book. She is both an outstanding educator and a spiritual friend.

I owe a debt of gratitude to my older son, Billy, for his constructive ideas during the process of writing the book and for his constant love and support. Likewise, my thanks to my other two children, Suzie and David; your love and interest have always been there as well.

I am very much indebted to Erin Milnes for her fine work in editing the book and gentleness in dealing with the author.

I would like to thank Rev. Keith Krim for his support and encouragement.

To the many friends, patients, and religious who in their own ways have added an entirely new spiritual dimension to my professional and personal life, I thank you. You know who you are.

Thanks to Betty FitzPatrick for her typing during the early phases of the book's development.

Last, but by no means least, I thank my wife, Aline, for all she has brought to my life: that "joy that comes in the morning"—hope transformed into reality.

Introduction

If someone dropped a china plate out of a tenth floor window and it landed on the cement pavement below, the plate would be shattered into many pieces. This was the way I felt several years ago when I found myself confronting an unexpected divorce. Were this same plate to be reassembled, it would be a different item indeed. Putting together the many scattered pieces would take much time and diligence. But more importantly, the plate would be transformed, be different, be unique, and it might very well be more useful than before.

This book depicts a time of brokenness in my life, a time of "picking up the pieces." It is a story of my journey through a very dark tunnel—a place of dying and at the same time a place of reaching the deepest center of my being. The pain, the feelings of rejection, and the sense of failure during the ensuing few years were ultimately replaced by an inner healing and peace, creating a new spiritual dimension to my personal life and medical practice. I came to more fully experience what Paul said about dying to the old self (Romans 6.6–8). I realized that until my own inner healing took place, I would not enjoy God's gift of inner peace. Similarly, without inner peace, I would not be an effective channel for healing the needs of others, and after all, being a physician, I was supposed to be a healer. As Christians, our goal is to glorify God in our lives. This is clearly stated in scripture by Matthew:

> You are the light of the world. . . . let your light shine before men, that they may see your good deeds and praise your Father in heaven.
>
> Matthew 5.14, 16

People everywhere are hurting. Regardless of their socio-economic backgrounds, people are crying out to be listened to, to be cared for, to be touched. Patients, especially, want an ear that listens and a heart that understands and is attentive to them. We physicians must react with compassion and not just sympathy. We have to lighten our patients' yokes. We have to be present with our hearts and not just our scientific minds. Chuck Swindoll, a noted Christian writer and speaker, touched on this when he wrote, "When people are hurting, they need much more than an accurate analysis and diagnosis."[1] Our spiritual natures must be able to communicate with their spiritual natures—we must attempt to feel a oneness with each patient.

In so many cases, the great advances of medical bioengineering have resulted in separating us even further from our patients. We are traveling down the road of high technology while ignoring the spiritual side of caring. Scientific advances, which have helped save so many lives, have all too often replaced hands-on patient care. Patients are physically cured but not emotionally or spiritually healed. Some medical schools are attempting to remedy this situation by devoting a few hours to the "human side" of patient care. This is a start, but it hardly scratches the surface.

As you read some of my patients' case histories, I believe you will notice the bonding between my patients and me brought about by the power of the Holy Spirit. Physician-patient rapport and communication are important in this age of declining respect for doctors and of often unrealistic expectations of patients for complete cures, resulting in rising malpractice premiums. I don't suggest that we ignore modern medical technology but that we be more attentive to patients' spiritual needs.

At the present time, I pray with one or two patients every day, and frequently patients pray for me as well. Praying this way has resulted in a new joy in my life, not present in the previous twenty years. I have a consciousness of a presence in all encounters. This presence speaks and acts through me in a way I never dreamed possible. My openness to God's presence within me at all times led to the realization that he is also inside of others, even though they may not think of themselves as children of God. This openness to God's presence also led to a spiritual connection between my patients and me, which had a

---

[1] Chuck Swindoll, *Growing Strong in the Seasons of Life* (Portland, OR: Multnomah Press, 1983), 238.

positive impact on communication and healing and has led to many miraculous recoveries, both large and small. Many of these experiences will be described in this book.

Healers, be they health-care providers, clergy, teachers, or laypeople helping others, all can suffer from exhaustion. Giving one's energies in the service of others, day in and day out, is enervating and can lead to physical, emotional, and spiritual depletion, and even discouragement. Not only are healers subject to burnout but so are people in other vocations as well. In chapter 6, I will list some of the ways I have found essential for keeping the spiritual fires burning as well as for keeping that much needed inner peace. It is impossible to be one of God's servants in the world—a world that is hurting and crying out for compassion—by our strength alone. We need spiritual sustenance and God's strength and guidance.

Although much of this book is written from a Christian perspective, we must remember, regardless of our own religious tradition, we are all children of the same Being.

1

The Journey Begins

The Early Years

As I look back now, I see that God's love and guidance were ever-present in my life, even in my earliest years. I was fortunate to have parents who affirmed me every step along the way. We hugged and expressed openly our affection for each other. This undoubtedly had an important impact on my life, and engendered bonding and trust at a very early age. My parents appreciated me for what I was, praised me when I succeeded, and never chided me for doing poorly as long as I did the best that I could under the circumstances.

I was a member of a sandlot football team when I was about ten years old. We all had different uniforms and didn't have a coach, but we practiced in a neighbor's backyard. We were just a bunch of kids who loved the game. One day we played against an organized team, on a real football field. The opposition all had the same uniforms, and seemed very talented and well coached. They beat us 53 to 0. My father watched that game, and despite the debacle, at the end of the game he reassured me by saying, "Son, when you hit the line carrying the ball, though you didn't go very far, I could still see your legs moving up and down despite having half of the opposition on your back."

When I was thirteen, my father died of a chronic liver ailment. He died at home after being ill for many weeks. My heart broke each night as I heard him moan with pain in a semi-stupor. To see this man who was so athletic and healthy waste away under my eyes and finally die, deeply jaundiced in liver coma, devastated me. This loss left my mother, a schoolteacher and later an elementary school supervisor, alone and with a very small salary. I had no brothers or sisters. We moved to her parents' home. We read *Daily Word* (a monthly publication of the Unity School of Christianity that includes a message for every day of the year and stresses a positive attitude toward life's challenges based on the knowledge of God's love and perfect plan for each of his children) every morning at breakfast for the next several years until I left my home to join the service at age seventeen. I began to sense God's presence almost daily during those trying years. The service led eventually to college, medical school, postgraduate training, more time in the service, this time as a Navy physician, and finally married life and starting a practice.

During this chain of events, I always kept in close contact with my mother whether by mail, telephone, or visits on weekends or holidays. We each had our own *Daily Word* and shared the reading when together. From these daily devotions we learned the power of affirmation prayer, which is thanking God for things not seen or events not yet witnessed. When I was a teenager, we often discussed how we should spend our money. Usually something practical, such as a vacuum cleaner, was chosen over a "luxury" item such as a new radio. There was one time, however, when we decided that fun and relaxation can take precedence over practical concerns. We bought a TV instead of a dishwasher, and the fun of watching good shows was well worth washing dishes by hand for another year. Times were not easy, and I'll always remember when my mother remarked, years later, that she had pawned her rings in order to have enough cash to buy me a present the first Christmas after my father died.

Love Letters to God

My mother not only made use of affirmation prayers in her daily life, but she frequently went one step further and wrote down these prayers in the form of letters to God. After writing the prayer, she signed her first name, placed the prayer in a dated envelope, sealed it, and placed it in the bottom drawer of her desk or in the family Bible. In other words, she turned it over to God.

These letters were really "affirmations"—prayers that thanked God for his perfect answer to concerns at work or at home or to financial needs before the answer actually manifested itself. I distinctly remember her reading me one of her letters that thanked our Lord for her new position as elementary school supervisor of the five Orange Public Schools, a position that had just been created. Shortly after writing the letter, she was offered the job. She went on to write a basic reading book, which was published, while studying at night school for a Ph.D. and tutoring children in reading after work in our home. She turned her life over to God, trusted in his all-providing grace, and acknowledged her blessings with daily thanksgiving.

Some of her letters concerned her health, as her career in education was closing and time for retirement was fast approaching. She was suffering from transient small strokes that caused her to fall down suddenly. She would get up and smile and dismiss it by saying that she must have tripped over something. She now lived fifty miles away from our family, and so she prayed she would be able to sell the old house and move near us. Her prayers were answered when she sold the house and moved next door to us. Her beloved three-year-old grandson, Billy, visited her daily. Her life appeared to be full. Tragically, she suffered from further strokes that left her badly disabled requiring supervised nursing care for the last few years before she died. Despite her misfortunes, my mother's letters were rarely concerned with requests. Instead, her faith in God's perfect plan led her to pray affirmation prayers most of the time. All concerns, large or small, were given over to God's will rather than her own will, knowing that, over time, her solution could very well turn out to be the worst one.

In retreats in recent years, the retreat leader has asked us to write down on paper all our major burdens and place the paper on the church altar, giving the paper and its contents over to God's grace. This practice reminds me of my mother's practice of turning her own "love letters" over to her dearest Lord.

A few years ago, after she had been gone for about ten

years, I picked up the old, large, and heavy family Bible, and out fell several of her letters. They were written in the 1940s, 1950s, and 1960s. To my joy, each prayer had been answered as she had hoped, or it had turned out better than anticipated. My mother's prayers were for me to receive the following:

1. A scholarship to a private school noted for its college preparatory program
2. Safety in the Pacific in World War II
3. Two financial aid scholarships and a job in Princeton as an undergraduate
4. Funds for medical school (A neighbor unexpectedly offered to pay my entire tuition for four years. I was able to pay this money back in full ten years later, a few years before he died.)
5. A good internship and residency in New York City
6. A good place to practice
7. A family with a wife and a home

Everything my mother prayed for was given to me. The Lord's thread connected me from one event to the next. If ever there were visible proof of answered prayers, those letters were indeed a testimony. I have also written letters, over the past years, sealed and dated them and later, perhaps months or years, opened them. My prayers were also answered. Many times God's answers differed from my own wishes, but when I examined the situation later on I realized that his answers were better than my own wishes.

Finally my mother died, having seen all three grandchildren born, me settled in practice, her home sold, and a new home established near us. Her prayers had all been answered. Her life was a series of successes, as a teacher and author, in graduate work, and in school promotion from first grade teacher to elementary supervisor. Virtually each step along the way had been handed over to God through a letter. Once the prayer was tucked between the pages of the family Bible, she let go and trusted that he would hear her concerns and answer the prayer according to his wisdom. Each letter was an act of faith. As Paul said, "Now faith is being sure of what we hope for and certain of what we do not see" (Hebrews 11.1).

I strongly recommend writing "love letters" to the Lord. You will find a living testimony to the Lord's grace in his answers to prayers, prayers written in your own handwriting! I have suggested this practice to a number of patients, and the following is just one case in many.[1]

Not too long ago, Sam, a sixty-year-old man, mentioned to me three major concerns in his life. His first concern was for his health. He was scheduled for open heart surgery due to severe coronary artery disease. He required several nitroglycerine tablets and other cardiac medications daily to help him overcome frequent bouts of chest pain. His life-style was definitely hampered by this condition in that the slightest exertion or emotional upset evoked chest discomfort. He was fearful of the upcoming open-heart surgery as well as of the possibility of a heart attack before surgery.

Sam's second concern was that he might lose his job because his company was being merged with a larger firm. He was afraid that if he did lose his job, no one would hire him because of his age. He was not unlike so many people in mid-life who are vulnerable to losing their jobs because of mergers and acquisitions.

Sam's third concern was for his stepson's mental health. Sam had remarried several years before, and the marriage was successful in all aspects except for a poor relationship with his teenage stepson, Paul. Paul suffered from a complexity of emotional problems that occasionally were severe enough for hospitalization and intensive psychotherapy.

At the conclusion of our office visit, we prayed about each of his major concerns, as Sam was inherently a very spiritual person. We both acknowledged that God is always with us. I told him that the hard part often is just to turn our concerns over to God and to trust in his grace and guidance. I mentioned how my mother and I both had written down our concerns in the form of a letter to God. I suggested that he place the letter in an envelope with the date and the word "personal" written on it,

---

[1] Throughout the book, names, ages, and occasionally circumstances have been altered to protect patient confidentiality.

seal the envelope, and place it out of sight, in a Bible or desk drawer, for example. I told him not to look at it for many months, or even years, leaving it in the hands of our Lord. He agreed to do this when he returned home.

Several months passed. Sam returned to the office for a routine visit. He said he found his letter while going through his desk drawer and had opened and read it only a few days earlier. There were the prayers, affirmation prayers, in his own handwriting, thanking God in advance, knowing that all three concerns would be answered according to God's will. The cardiac surgery went well, and he now requires fewer medications than before and is able to do many more activities without chest pains. He lost his job, but his old company retained him to do part-time consulting, allowing him to enjoy more flexible hours. Another firm also hired him for consulting work, again with flexible hours. The result was that his income increased, and he now has more time to help his stepson in the house-building business. Sam spends one or two days a week helping his stepson and actually enjoys the physical activity. His relationship with Paul has greatly improved. Paul, in turn, is doing better psychologically. As we reflected upon how the Lord had answered his needs, we rejoiced and said a prayer of thanksgiving.

Natural Meditations

I have always loved nature and have experienced the wonder of all creation during times I have spent walking along the seashore, in the quiet woods, or just smelling the soil in the backyard after a heavy rainstorm. I bought an old farm twenty-five years ago located in the hills of Pennsylvania that has been, and continues to be, a place for retreat and spiritual development, complete with country noises, clear air, and starry skies. At the farm I become conscious of changes in the seasons. Before long, my own body rhythms become part of nature's rhythms. I develop a sense of unity with the surroundings. During times of quiet meditation in places like the farm, I experience a oneness with all of God's creation, a sense of belonging to a plan that God himself has for all living things, including myself.

Soon after acquiring the farm, I began a project to plant pine tree seedlings—five hundred a year. I planted them on an April weekend every year for ten years. Most of these seedlings ended up in an old apple orchard. The apple trees had died, and the ground was covered with briars and wild rose bushes. Even to this day, I never miss an opportunity to walk among the pine trees, encouraging them and enjoying their eighteen-inch per year growth. Many of the trees are now over thirty feet tall. I love to sit quietly beneath this cathedral of trees in all seasons. One can easily come into the presence of our Lord in places like this, quietly meditating and experiencing the wonder of his world and its beauty. Isaiah 55.12–13 describes perfectly the farm and God's everlasting presence there:

> You will go out in joy
> and be led forth in peace;
> The mountain and hills
> will burst into song before you,
> and all the trees of the field
> will clap their hands.
> Instead of the thornbush will grow
> the pine tree,
> and instead of briers the myrtle
> will grow.
> This will be for the Lord's renown,
> for an everlasting sign,
> which will not be destroyed.

Like my vacations at the farm, many ocean crossings on troopships, first as a deck officer and later as a ship's medical officer, gave me ample time to reflect on the Lord's beauty manifested in peaceful sunrises, sunsets, star-filled nights, and even the raging storms frequently found in the North Atlantic. I experienced virtually the entire spectrum of nature's offerings during my multiple Atlantic, Caribbean, and Pacific crossings.

Storms have a mystical beauty. During stormy times at sea, you point the bow into the waves so as not to be broadside and risk capsizing. You put the ship's engines on "slow ahead" in order to steer the vessel. After that, you sit back and wait, trusting in the calm that is sure to follow. Likewise, by confronting our crises head-on and trusting in God's plan for each of us, we can be assured of his peace in the end. Both storms and peaceful, beautiful days at sea have counterparts in our lives. The hand of God is outstretched to us in all conditions of our lives. We must be open to this and trust him.

Zipped-up Professional

The years moved on and in 1960, when I finally had finished the many years of preparation to become a physician, I married and started the private practice of medicine in Princeton, New Jersey. I soon had a very busy practice, three lovely children, a harmonious house, and an apparently happy marriage.

For the following twenty years I was the picture of a hardworking physician, doing my very best and trying to keep abreast of scientific advances in internal medicine and cardiology. However, I did not allow myself to become very involved with anything of a spiritual nature. Instead, I wore my white coat, stood alongside the hospital bed, rarely touched a patient except for the examination required in the routine physical, and undoubtedly talked more than I listened to what my patients were struggling to tell me concerning their private lives, which was often the real cause of the "disease."

I felt that it was sufficient to make a diagnosis and to treat it. Anything else going on inside the patient was out of bounds or at best was handled by a tranquilizer or a superficial word of encouragement. If this didn't work, I often suggested the patient see a psychologist or psychiatrist. I was basically a "zipped-up" professional, both unable and unwilling to open my heart and "take off the white coat" in order to enter into what was troubling the patient's soul. I might add that a good number of my colleagues seemed to be working in a similar mold.

I went to church most Sundays, read a daily Christian missal at breakfast with the children, and seemed to be living a comfortable life. Then something strange happened after about fifteen years of practice: I found myself having a seemingly unquenchable thirst for books about the Holy Spirit. C. S. Lewis touched on this innate hunger for our Lord:

Apparently then, our lifelong nostalgia, our longing to be reunited with something in the universe from which we now feel cut off, to be inside of some door which we have always seen from the outside is no mere neurotic fancy, but the truest index of our real situation. . . . We do not want merely to see beauty, but God knows even that is beauty enough. We want something else . . . to be united with the beauty we see, to pass into it, to receive it into ourselves, to bathe in it, to become part of it.[2]

This was how the Lord was pulling me—to be enveloped by him and become part of him. This pull was so intense that although I was busy studying for cardiology specialty examinations, I found that I spent at least half of my available time reading books on spirituality. Much of what I read dealt with Christian healing. It was strange, in hindsight, that God seemed to be laying a groundwork for me, a resource for the fires that were about to come, and it was equally strange that he was directing me toward literature dealing with the healing of life's hurts and the necessity of treating the "whole person." By "whole person" I mean our spiritual nature and its effect on illness, in addition to the time-honored physical and emotional side of illness.

Looking back, I see that God had secretly placed a reservoir of future strength alongside of me at that time—I had learned Transcendental Meditation (TM), which led to Christian centering prayer. I had been given a spiritual director, several very close friends, a farm, and a loving relationship with my three teenage children. It had become almost second nature for me to employ affirmation prayer on a daily basis and in all sorts of conditions. In this affirmation prayer I thank God for being present and for the knowledge and faith of his perfect plan in my life. I had no idea that he had a "Big Bang" (a major crisis) waiting just around the corner, that was to drastically change my life. The Lord had placed a support system on the sidelines ready to be called upon at a moment's notice.

---

[2] C. S. Lewis, *The Weight of Glory and Other Addresses* (New York: Macmillan, 1949) 15–16.

Paul Tournier, M.D., a Swiss psychiatrist, touched upon God's presence in our lives when he wrote:

> God guides us despite our uncertainties and our vagueness, even through our failings and mistakes. . . . Only afterwards, as we look back over the way we have come and reconsider certain important moments in our lives in the light of all that has followed them, or when we survey the whole progress of our lives do we experience the feeling of having been led without knowing it, the feeling that God has mysteriously guided us. [3]

---

[3] Paul Tournier, *Reflections* (Philadelphia: Westminster Press, 1976), 123.

2

Crisis: The Divorce

The Announcement

I'll never forget that June evening when suddenly my (now) ex-wife mentioned divorce. It came like a bolt of lightning out of the blue. We had been together for twenty years, twenty happy years I thought. We were successfully raising three children and were achieving some success in our careers as well as working toward our individual educational goals. I was making advances in my profession, and she had written two books, was actively studying for further degrees, and was a successful tennis player ranked in women's singles in the Middle Atlantic States.

We attempted marriage counseling, but it was unsuccessful. Communication, or lack of it, seemed to be at the the root of the problem. I certainly was not "tuned in" finely enough to catch what was going on. I was too busy providing for the family and building a practice and, in hindsight, was spending a disproportionate share of free time with the kids, playing or wrapped up in their concerns, rather than with my wife and her inner concerns. Regardless of my intentions, I'm sure I contributed significantly to the problem, since in all domestic crises of this sort no one partner is totally without blame.

11

Despite the reconciliation attempts, living at home while waiting several months for the separation agreement to be drawn up was extremely painful. We were hardly speaking, and an atmosphere of apathy mixed with anger had developed. Added to the discomfort was the new reality of separate bedrooms, the disappearance of the engagement and wedding rings from her finger, and the constant tension. Many nights I slept only a few hours. Fortunately I kept busy during the day at work, though I felt very fatigued. I remember being still awake at 3:00 a.m., going downstairs, and sitting on the couch, full of grief and worry about the effects the divorce would have on the children. I sat one day with my thirteen-year-old son (the youngest child), trying to explain that we must have the same faith a farmer does after he plants his seeds. We must trust, like he does, that the seed will sprout into a full plant, that God will hear us, and that in the end all will be well. I'm sure the children never doubted that both their parents loved them completely, but could they handle this situation? Would it scar them? Would I be able to cope? Everyone experiences some unexpected tragedies during the course of a lifetime. I had many tearful talks with each child, interspersed with hugs, during the early days following the divorce announcement.

The nights were very bleak and long, and the days were lonely, worrisome, and weary. I was working a full schedule with only three or four hours of sleep per night. The atmosphere had been transformed into one of grief, frustration, and anger. My ex-wife was reading books about "mid-life crisis," and I was trying to seek inner strength and peace by reading books about the Holy Spirit. It seemed to me that neither of us appreciated what the other was reading. I remember the sinking feeling I had once when I heard a popular song on the radio asking, "Where are the clowns?" But with each passing week, reconciliation became progressively more unlikely, and I finally moved to a one-bedroom apartment several miles away and signed a one-year lease. This was a turning point. I had finally come to accept that I was now a single parent and vowed that this would be the start of putting my life back together again.

Loss of a spouse, whether by death or divorce, is always painful. In the case of divorce, the additional problem of rejection must be dealt with. Community support may be somewhat slim. In addition to these problems, I felt a sense of failure, a loss of self-worth, a lack of self-confidence, guilt, and humiliation. I remember reading John 16.22, "Now is your time of grief, but I will see you again and you will rejoice, and no one will take away your joy." When things looked black everywhere, I found consolation in those words. Would there really be joy for me some time in the future? Did I dare to trust in this passage?

I never before appreciated so much the love, concern, and caring of friends. One friend, a busy president of his own corporation, called daily from New York and even waited on the phone when I was seeing patients. When I asked him why he called so frequently, he calmly said, "Because I love you and want to make sure you're all right." Over the next few years other friends gave me extended invitations to visit or stay for dinner during the major holidays, when I otherwise would have been alone. A pastor of one of the local churches, at the conclusion of a Sunday service, saw me leave from the back of the church. He left his congregation standing in the door and ran across the street, hugged me, and invited me to spend Thanksgiving at his home rather than alone in my apartment. By this action I could see he was truly a man of love. Some of my patients began praying for my needs at the conclusion of their office visits. A new dimension to our traditional doctor-patient relationship developed as we became prayer partners for each other's needs. Today, when my patients, suffering the pains of divorce, come to me, I can help them by sharing my story. No one has better credentials to help than someone who has been there. I know what it is like to experience the pain, and that knowledge is powerful!

In an editorial in the *New England Journal of Medicine*, "Healing by the Fundamentals," Walter W. Benjamin, Ph.D., writes:

> Literature is full of the image of the "wounded healer,"
> in which life and death are found in the same figure.
> Thornton Wilder, Unamuno, Camus, and other au-
> thors have discovered that healers have power if they

have wounds.

Faith in Jesus Christ, the Wounded One with stigmata, has brought healing to millions who believe that God identifies with the sufferer in his pain and in his terror confronting death.

Objectively, care aims at dispensing medical knowledge. Nonetheless, subjectively, it is mediated through personality. You may not wish it, but some of your patients regard you as their pastor or priest. A discrete sharing of your wounds—your views of life and death, courage and faith, and joy and tragedy—may be very appropriate. Don't underestimate what it might do for your patient.[1]

No Pain, No Gain

A comment frequently heard in athletic circles is "No pain, no gain." There is some truth in this. You have to train very hard to compete in most sports, and this training can entail pushing yourself to your physical and psychological limits. Similarly, painful life stresses can lead to spiritual growth. Situations like death or divorce may be devastating enough so as to soften our hard hearts and open us up to God's presence as we surrender for the first time total control of everything in our lives to his wisdom and guidance. This is a humbling experience and does not occur overnight.

There were more than enough opportunities for spiritual gain during the bleak days after the separation. First of all, I had to drop off my children at the home that I built and then drive back to my dark apartment alone, after having been part of a family for the previous twenty years. Try that for a few weeks! In order to chat with the children in person as much as possible, I would park in the street in front of the house to take them to

---

[1] Walter W. Benjamin, "Healing by the Fundamentals," *New England Journal of Medicine* 331(1984): 594–97.

school in the morning. My former neighbors would drive to work, see me, and wave, and I would feel awkward and crushed as I tried to smile and wave back.

Even the faithful dog felt the change and wondered why I didn't greet him every morning and night. He successfully jumped into my car through an open window more than once. Little did he know that dogs were not allowed in my apartment complex.

To help me feel more at home and because I did not have any of the children's baby pictures, the children put together, on a large piece of cardboard, a collage of about thirty pictures. Under each picture they wrote a thank you to me for being their father and for bringing love into their lives. I cried when they brought it to the apartment on Father's Day.

The wife of an old friend helped me decorate the apartment. It was a pleasant apartment, a second floor walk-up facing east, and was drenched with sun for most of the daylight hours. The children and their friends seemed to enjoy spending the night there. Frequently both couches were used as beds and often there were even a few of their friends sleeping on the living room floor. Small places seem to attract a spirit of closeness that large places miss. Have you ever wondered why people love to sit around and chat in a group in the kitchen when they could spread out in a living room? Anyway, the apartment was quite cozy and I found sitting on the balcony and watching the sunset or stars both peaceful and uplifting, and my friends and children did too.

After I moved into the apartment, I wanted to add to its warmth and coziness. The tiny balcony was a focal point. It became a peaceful place, and part of nature and the out-of-doors. All it needed was some flowers, which I placed all around it. I had a specially made canvas placed horizontally around the balcony about four feet high that served as a windbreaker and that gave some privacy as well. The balcony was sunny, and at sunset I could sit out there and enjoy the view of the beautiful woods in the distance and watch the stars begin to light up. The four-by-ten-foot balcony was a special place, and the children loved it. It served both as a garden and a small retreat center. I even placed a stone statue of St. Francis, standing peacefully, among some tall potted plants in one corner of this small arboretum.

Learning to cook was a new experience. In order to prevent a pizza from getting too cold, it seemed wise to keep it in the cardboard container and place it in the oven. I soon smelled smoke and pulled it out a moment before the whole box caught fire. Another time I placed a frozen entree, packaged in a plastic container, in the oven. As you can imagine, the plastic dish and food melted together. The kids had similar culinary disasters when they took turns being the chef from time to time. Following each disaster the chef was presented with the "Royal Order of the Plastic Dish," i.e., the remains of the distorted plastic food container. We all received this award more than once.

Shopping for food and going to the cleaners had to be done at lunch hour. I was surprised to see how many men were shopping for food, many of them married. I always managed to run into a few patients at the checkout counter, especially women, who complimented me on my newfound domestic abilities.

Other domestic chores, like mending shirts, sewing on buttons, pressing clothes, and doing laundry, brought back memories of my experience in the service.

Of course, I still had feelings of emptiness when going to church, sitting alone in the pew wondering what people were thinking, or going to parties or out to dinner without a partner. But with the passage of time, I felt I was surviving and began to feel I might even be prevailing. A transition slowly came about, with God's grace, from the loneliness of separation to the peace of being alone. It was during the quiet times that I could sense God's healing balm, especially when with him in prayer. At this time, I began setting aside one half hour every morning for reading scripture and meditating. I often turned to Psalm 37.23–24 for comfort. "If the Lord delights in a man's way, he makes his step firm; though he stumble, he will not fall, for the Lord upholds him with his hand." The words of Paul to the Romans also comforted me. "Be joyful in hope, patient in affliction, faithful in prayer" (Romans 12.12). In other words, it is important not to give up when trials come but to keep on praying.

I realized that God's constant thread was intertwined with mine all along my life's journey, when I heard this from Jeremiah,

> I have loved you with an
> everlasting love;
> I have drawn you with
> loving-kindness.

Jeremiah 31.3

3

The Search for Answers

A Transformation

It was only by experiencing the pain of divorce that I realized that I had been too caught up with my own worldly desires, ambitions, responsibilities, and pace of living, and that I hadn't allowed for any time to listen to what the Lord was trying to tell me. I hadn't let him become one with me or let him guide me. Slowly I realized that God speaks to us in many ways—through events, other people, our "small, inner voice," nature, dreams, and the church, to name a few. I realized that he let a crisis come into my life as still another way of getting my attention. I learned that the Lord has an overall plan for each of his children. But this child was not, evidently, following the path God wanted—I was not listening; I was not aware that I should be and should have been a channel for God's love. When heavy trials left me in a dark place with no one to turn to, when I came finally to depend on him totally for help, when I literally crawled to the cross, only then was I opening myself to God's love and grace. So many of us seem to have to go through the fires of pain and suffering before we totally give ourselves over.

I came across a sermon by John Wesley, founder of the Methodist Church, relating to a time of crisis (what he calls a "wilderness state"). The gist of the sermon seemed to be, "hang in there and keep praying"—a very important concept he learned early on.

> Above all, let them be instructed, when the storm is upon them, not to reason with the devil, but to pray; to pour out their souls before God, and show Him of their trouble....and God will then bear witness to His word, and bring their souls out of trouble. He will say, "Arise, shine; for thy light is come, and the glory of the Lord is risen upon thee." Yea, and that light, if thou walk humbly and closely with God, will "shine more and more unto the perfect day."[1]

Paul Vitz, a professor of psychology at New York University, in his book, *The Cult of Self-Worship*,[2] mentions how the "self-made man," the "self-sufficient" individual will thrive until he or she finds himself or herself crying out, "God help me," when caught in the middle of a major crisis. Ultimately comes the confession, "I can't do it alone—I need your help, O God." The old saying during World War II was, "There are no atheists in foxholes." When total control of one's life is lost as in such circumstances, it is not difficult to imagine the most self-sufficient person calling out to the Lord for help.

The psalmist aptly articulates this plea for help. "Give us aid against the enemy, for the help of man is worthless" (Psalm 60.11). The miracle is that God hears our cries, and we begin to grow in his grace. We are gradually transformed. We survive; we prevail; we are witnesses, and we then reach out to others—all through God's love and according to his plan for each of us.

William Barclay, the well-known Scottish minister and lecturer from the University of Glasgow, writes that at times of darkness and pain "sorrow can be one of two things to us. It can make us hard, bitter, resentful, rebellious against God. Or it can make us kinder, softer, more sympathetic. It can despoil us of our faith, or it can root faith even deeper."[3]

---

[1] John Wesley, Sermon XL, *Sermons on Several Occasions*, Vol. II (London: The Epworth Press, 1956), 262–63.

[2] Paul Vitz, *The Cult of Self-Worship* (Grand Rapids, MI: William B. Eerdmans Publishing Company, 1982), 104.

[3] William Barclay, *The Gospel of Luke*, The Daily Study Bible Series, revised edition (Philadelphia: Westminster Press, 1975), 27.

The Answer: Christ and Inner Healing

In my search for answers, I traveled several paths. I remember taking a course in Transcendental Meditation (TM) a few years before the divorce. I learned how to "center" by repeating over and over a word, called a mantra, while sitting in a relaxed manner. Now I can attain this inner state of peace by other means, e.g., saying the Jesus Prayer or a line of scripture. When I reach the center, I am quiet and listen to God speaking by way of that "small inner voice" inside me. Sometimes I say a prayer, or am still, or praise him, or am thankful.

I also took a couple of EST courses before the divorce. The message I received there was that I should create my own world and be self-assertive. The EST courses lacked anything spiritual. The emphasis seemed to be on making things happen, taking control. Undoubtedly, the Lord won't move a parked car, and there comes a time for making decisions and acting on them. There is, therefore, some worth in taking control and making things happen. Despite the value of taking charge, it made more sense to me at that time to learn to be quiet and learn to listen to what God might be saying to me, to pray about matters and then act. So often we are rushing around so fast we don't make room in our daily lives for quiet, prayerful time. Mother Teresa feels silence (both internal and external) is essential in order for God to hear us and speak to us. She said, "God is the friend of silence. We need to find God, but we cannot find Him in noise, in excitement." She goes on to say, "The more we receive in our silent prayer, the more we can give in our active life. We need this silence to touch souls. The essential thing is not what we say but what God says to us and what He says through us."[4]

Christianity doesn't condemn the human self, but it is only when the human self takes precedence over the spiritual self that there is room for conflict. *The Word*, a Christian monthly, stated recently, "All Christians must learn that 'self' has to die to make room for Jesus to live within them. 'Self' refers to the whole complex of forces, drives, and energies within us which are opposed to God. The natural life in us must die; it is incapable of reformation or renewal."[5] By becoming more Christ-

---

[4] Mother Teresa of Calcutta, *The Love of Christ: Spiritual Counsels*, Georges Gorrée and Jean Barbier, eds. (San Francisco: Harper and Row, 1982), 8,9.

[5] *The Word*, Anthony Bosnick, ed., 30 August 1987.

like, we are not taking control but surrendering to God and letting him work through us. We "let go and let God."

Sharing with Others

Retreats played a large role in my spiritual journey in those days and continue to do so. One of the earlier retreats in which I participated was given by Bishop Lance Webb, a retired Methodist bishop in Florida. Bishop Webb has been a leader in the Disciplined Order of Christ (DOC), founded in 1945, for many years. Members of this great organization vow to set aside time daily for prayer and scripture reading. They commit themselves to a life-style emphasizing eight disciplines: obedience, simplicity, humility, frugality, generosity, truthfulness, purity, and charity. Members also are obligated to belong to an organized church and to respect and use wisely the earth's resources.

The retreat with Bishop Webb lasted several days. There were about twenty of us in the group. It was during this retreat that I first learned to share my burdens with a close and caring group of strangers, to accept their prayers for me, and to be able to lay hands on and to pray, in turn, for others' needs. I remember how surprised I was one day when the Bishop turned to me and asked me to pray for him! Even bishops have needs like the rest of us. This idea came to me as a minor revelation.

Subsequent retreats over the past several years included a five-day stay in the beautiful Colorado Rockies. This retreat is directed toward the needs of clergy and health-care providers; it is run by the School of Pastoral Care and sponsored by the Episcopal Church of Colorado. The natural beauty of the mountains blends with the inner beauty of those who are present. Inner healing was and continues to be at the center of all the retreats I've had the privilege to attend.

I'll never forget taking part in the annual Catholic Charismatic Conference several years ago in South Bend. Can you imagine ten thousand participants inside a huge auditorium lifting up their arms to the Lord and singing and praising God? This kind of experience is bound to make the most uptight Episcopalian, like I used to be, really loosen up. I found that I had to be unzipped before I could be vulnerable enough to pray and share with others. This experience, as well as occasional Sunday evening services at a local Assembly of God Church, enabled me to actually experience the Holy Spirit at work within a group and, in a new way, within myself as well. Becoming a part of an entire congregation singing wonderful hymns with arms raised up, praising God, was a new and moving experience for me, even though I felt uneasy in the beginning because I had come from a more conservative religious tradition. The whole church seemed to vibrate with the presence of the Holy Spirit. This experience of being unzipped helped me to be more open to all religious traditions and to be less inhibited when dealing with my patients' emotions.

Early on, I joined the Christian Medical Foundation (CMF), a group of about three thousand physicians mainly from North America, but also from the Caribbean and Europe. At CMF meetings we pray, share practice experiences, and listen to professional papers presented from all medical specialties. We also sing hymns, which I greatly appreciate. CMF members try to address spirituality in addition to the standard medical concerns in their practices.

I attended a weekend retreat run by Fr. Gerald Ruane of the Sacred Heart Institute of Healing and was retreat leader the following year. The mission of this retreat was to heal the healers. One of the highlights was a trip to a local school on the last Sunday afternoon of the retreat. At the school, bus loads of people had lined up, many in wheelchairs or with crutches. We broke into small groups and prayed for them. This event greatly touched me and showed both the power of prayer and the strong faith of these believers as they patiently waited for God's healing, using us as channels of his love.

The Miracle of Prayer

By the end of a few years I began experiencing, in ever increasing numbers, the miracles of prayer in practice. As C. S. Lewis said in his definition of miracles, "But in Christianity, the more we understand what God it is who is said to be present and the purpose for which He is said to have appeared, the more credible the miracles become."[6]

---

[6] C. S. Lewis, *Miracles* (New York: Macmillan, 1960), 133.

I began to see how many patients were hurting or carrying heavy burdens in their hearts. To see the value of prayer incorporated into standard medical therapy was awesome. I will expand on this with many examples in the next few chapters. At this time I was on a few panels on prayer and inner healing at the Princeton Theological Seminary as a guest of Sr. Miriam Murphy, Ph.D., who, through the years, had become both a friend and spiritual guide.

I was asked to give a talk, one Sunday, at the nine and eleven o'clock services in a church in Connecticut 150 miles away and to lead a forum between the two services on the subject of inner healing and prayer. I was able to relate this subject to my personal life and private practice. (Having come from three generations of preachers, all based in New England, it was by God's grace I wasn't felled by a brick loosened by one of my ancestors when he found "Haynes, the Physician" in a pulpit!)

I participated in a number of retreats dedicated to healing, days of reflection, a special day of healing by the Linn brothers (Jesuit priests), and frequent lunches with my friend, Sr. Miriam. All of these activities continue to be invaluable in my search for and finding of God's will for my life.

Books, tapes, prayer groups, and church fellowship with special emphasis on the Eucharist were and continue to be important in my search and walk along life's road.

Up to this time of my life the scriptures had not been very relevant to much of my day-to-day routine, but during these early years of my transition they became alive. These writings from ancient times suddenly became very applicable to my life in the twentieth century. Passages from Ephesians and Corinthians spoke to me of new beginnings. "You were taught … to put off your old self … and to put on the new self, created to be like God in true righteousness and holiness" (Ephesians 4.22–24). "Therefore, if anyone is in Christ, he is a new creation; the old has gone, the new has come!" (2 Corinthians 5.17)

I realized that God never leaves us in our dark valleys. I learned to accept his power, his love, and his grace and learned to turn my problems over to him. I learned to rely on him and to trust him.

D. Elton Trueblood described beautifully the point of experiencing God and his works in our lives:

> There are many persons who not only desire the assurance that there is One at the heart of all things who cares for the values about which we care most at our best moments; they also report that they have had an experience of fellowship with Him. . . . And this One whom they believe they have known at first hand they call God. They believe many more things about Him, but the chief glory of their lives arises from the fact that they have met Him.[7]

This is not to imply that this is the end of my chapter or story, nor does it mean I will have smooth sailing from now on. Life is dynamic, changing, with daily needs, hurts, and anxieties as well as joy. Today I believe that God is constantly creating and re-creating all of us, wooing us to let him become increasingly more a part of our being, thus gradually transforming us to be more like his son. The more we recognize this the more it becomes a reality. This process of transformation and reconciliation with God, then, allows us also to be channels for reconciliation for God's people in the world around us.

My whole journey for answers has been one of shifting from "my way" to "God's way," which is quite the opposite of the way of self-assertion.

As strange as it may sound, our sufferings are great opportunities. We are forced to give up trying to control every aspect of our lives. Instead we allow God to guide us, as a stream guides a canoe. We steer to avoid the rocks, but let the stream take us where it's going. It can be very tiring paddling upstream, and, besides, you probably won't get anywhere.

Martin Luther King, Jr., learned firsthand of God's presence in life's darkest hour. He wrote:

> Recognizing the necessity of suffering, I have tried to make of it a virtue. The agonizing moments through which I have passed during the last few years con-

---

[7] D. Elton Trueblood, *The Essence of Spiritual Religion* (New York: Harper & Brothers, 1936), 9–10.

vinced me of the reality of a personal God. In the midst of outer dangers, I have felt an inner calm. In the midst of lonely days and dreary nights, I have heard an inner voice saying, "Lo, I will be with you."[8]

The Bible also tells us of God's comforting presence.

> Pray continually; give thanks in all circumstances this is God's will for you in Christ Jesus.
>
> 1 Thessalonians 5.17–18

> I am the light of the world. Whoever follows me will never walk in darkness, but will have the light of life.
>
> John 8.12

> In my distress I called to the Lord;
> I cried to my God for help.
> From his temple he heard my voice;
> my cry came before him, into his
> ears.
>
> Psalm 18.6

> The Lord is close to the
> brokenhearted
> and saves those who are crushed
> in spirit.
>
> Psalm 34.18

The grief, anger, and difficult chore of forgiveness that so frequently follow divorce cannot be handled by you alone. The support of friends and professional help are not only helpful but

---

[8] Martin Luther King, Jr., *Strength to Love* (Philadelphia: Fortress Press, 1981), 154.

often crucial. Nevertheless, it is the knowledge of God's love and peace, brought about by daily prayer, that can never be overestimated. Doris Donnelly mentions in her book, *Forgiveness*, that you can remain chained to spiritual or physical hurts.[9] The wounds have a power over us for years. She makes the point that forgiveness is the only way to break the chain and thus not be led by wounds and anger but by a stronger power through grace. It is important to forgive yourself as well as the one you feel has wounded you in order to get on with your life.

In time the answers had become very clear. The Lord was always there; he had never abandoned me but had guided me along his many paths, speaking through many people and circumstances.

As William Barclay so beautifully puts it, "He who called him to the steep road will be with him every step of the way and be there at the end to meet him."[10] Over the next few years healing progressed, joy returned, and I was ready to reach out and be a channel for healing for others in a way I never before dreamed possible.

Psalm 30.11–12 filled me with hope.

> You turned my wailing into
>   dancing;
> you removed my sackcloth and
>   clothed me with joy,
> that my heart may sing to you and
>   not be silent.
> O Lord my God, I will give you
>   thanks forever.

Psalm 66.19–20 jumped out of scripture and grabbed me.

> . . . but God has surely listened
>   and heard my voice in prayer.
> Praise be to God,
>   who has not rejected my prayer
>   or withheld his love from me!

---

[9] Doris Donnelly, *Forgiveness* (New York: Macmillan, 1979), 72.

[10] William Barclay, *The Gospel of Luke*, The Daily Study Bible Series, revised edition (Philadelphia: Westminster Press, 1975), 197.

Not only did scripture jump out and become more meaningful but the hymnal did as well. This was especially true of the fourth stanza of Hymn 636:

When through fiery trial thy pathway shall lie
My grace, all sufficient, shall by thy supply
The flame shall not hurt thee; I only design
Thy dross to consume and thy gold to refine.[11]

---

[11] *The Hymnal 1982* (New York: The Church Hymnal Corp., 1985), Hymn 636.

4

Reaching Out: Being a Channel for Healing and Reconciliation

Praying with Others

When life's wounds are being healed and we have seen what the Lord has done in our own lives, we can reach out with a thankful heart to help others. Prayer is a powerful tool in this regard. However, praying with others was not an easy step for me.

There were three stages in my journey, not unlike three rungs of a ladder. Each rung was separated by many weeks and months. The first stage consisted of the ability to tell patients when they were discharged from the hospital that I had prayed for them at home during their hospital stay. This took great courage on my part, because of the unorthodoxy of prayer as an adjunct to the standard medical treatment. Just the thought of mentioning it was frightening.

I had never encountered a course in medical school that mentioned the spiritual nature of a patient, nor had I encountered any physician who was willing to share his or her feelings regarding praying with patients. That does not mean that this form of caring was not practiced, but it does mean that it was probably too personal for the physicians to share with their students.

The scientific method (the reproducibility of any treatment modality) was and continues to be held as the standard by which to measure the effectiveness of treatment. How can you standardize the effects of prayer? Can you measure these effects? Can you do double-blind crossover studies to evaluate prayer's effectiveness as you do with new drugs? Can you quantify the power of the Holy Spirit and relate this to both physical, emotional, and spiritual healing? I knew my colleagues had many concerns about the propriety of prayer as an adjunct to medical treatment. Many believed that only clergy were qualified to pray with patients. I wasn't trained in a seminary. Besides, they wondered, how can prayer be an effective treatment and a physician a channel for God's healing, if the patient is not open to it? Because of these and many other reasons, I felt I was going against the tide of the scientific community, which caused me to feel very uneasy.

Besides the physician's attitude, the patient's conception of the role of the physician must be considered. The haunting question in the back of my mind was, and still is, "Is the patient open to prayer or is he or she totally closed to the idea?" How do you know whom to pray with or even talk with about prayer? God is with us, as I will show, every step of the way, and he gives us discernment, that is, the ability to pick up small clues, signals, or signs. Discernment allows you to know what form your prayer should take. I pray during virtually every patient encounter. The form it takes is dictated by the signals I receive. The prayer may be audible, accompanied by a touch or a hug, or may be totally inaudible. No matter what form, I am always asking God through this prayer, to heal, in his way, the pain of my patient.

After many weeks of gaining courage and confidence, I reached the second stage of my prayer journey. This consisted of the ability to tell the patients while they were still in the hospital that I was praying nightly for them. Whew! Another rung on the ladder! Though I never had any doubt that my goal was to be able to pray with my patients face to face, each step toward that goal was difficult because of my awareness of the potential disapproval of the patient. I was afraid of being rejected by patients who might criticize my approach or question my credentials for invoking prayer.

I reached the third, and final, stage many months later. This stage was the ability to ask patients, while at their bedside in the hospital, if we could pray together right then. Wow! What joy and what a feeling of oneness it was to be used, then and there, as a vehicle for God's power by laying on of hands and praying in the spirit. How thrilled I was to tell patients while they were still in the hospital and still not well enough to be discharged home, that I was praying nightly for them. Whew! The final rung of the ladder had been climbed! Formerly I had said things like "You are on my prayer list" or "I'm praying for you daily during my quiet time in the apartment" to certain hospital patients and a few office patients. Now I was able to discuss prayer with the patient while he or she was still in the hospital. At last, by reaching the third stage, I felt more complete in my role as a Christian physician. The uneasiness had vanished; the strength and peace received by the patients from the Holy Spirit were and are instantly perceptible!

Many times when praying with people you have only to ask the Holy Spirit to speak the words through you, and the Holy Spirit will give you the words of comfort that the patient needs. To my constant amazement, the words are always right on target—just what was needed, not too much or too little.

Invariably, when I approached prayer in this manner, both the patient and I received a blessing. The patient received a healing, and I, too, received one. It was a joy to have been used as a channel for this healing. Praying in the spirit this way allows God to lead your thoughts as you pray, while you yourself literally step out of the way to let him take over your words. You truly become a vehicle for his word.

A word of caution about asking someone to pray with you: Be sure you discern that he or she wants prayers. Some people feel uncomfortable with prayers, some just need the laying on of hands or a sensitive touch, and others just need an attentive ear. Your inner intuitive sense, your discernment, is important. You never want to steamroller prayers over someone who is not open and eager to receive this mode of healing.

When he or she prays for someone, the healer necessarily becomes vulnerable. Fortunately, over the past several years, I have never been refused by a coarse remark or have abruptly been told no. Everyone to date has welcomed our praying together. Following the prayer, the patient's usual response has been a deep sigh, some tears or outright crying (frequently joined by me), and a visible lifting of the burden as the patient hands this burden over to God. The patient gains a sense of inner peace and renewed hope. A relationship develops at a different level as the hospital course and subsequent office follow-up take on a spiritual dimension that is added to the professional dimension. The patient may exhibit new behavior in the form of a changed life-style, taking prescribed medications, and keeping appointments. Very often the patient and I say a prayer of thanksgiving for healing during the office follow-up after discharge from the hospital. Often, over subsequent office visits, we pray about other new problems that arise. We pray about his or her needs and, not infrequently, my needs as well. When discernment is used, praying with patients opens up an entirely new avenue for healing. When the physician acts as a vehicle for God's healing, as mentioned before, the patient and the physician both receive a blessing.

Whenever we pray with someone or are able to help someone, we must be clear that the healing and blessings that ensue come not from us but from our Lord. This thought is expressed by St. James:

> Is any one of you in trouble? He should pray. Is anyone happy? Let him sing songs of praise. Is any one of you sick? He should call the elders of the church to pray over him and anoint him with oil in the name of the Lord. And the prayer offered in faith will make the sick person well; the Lord will raise him up. If he has sinned, he will be forgiven.
>
> James 5.13–15

Seven cases follow that illustrate the major role prayer and healing can play in patient care.

A Struggle with Recurring Alcoholism

Alan is a sixty-six-year-old alcoholic. He had been a tail-gunner during World War II who was shot down and captured by the Japanese. He escaped from prison camp, found his way back to Allied lines, and began a drinking career that was to last for the next forty years. He had been admitted to the hospital many times—once or twice a year—for alcoholism and its related medical complications. He was a frail man and worked most days of the year as a clerk at a nearby plant. Many times he would telephone me and ask to be admitted to the hospital because he had just started to drink again after many months of sobriety. I would compliment him on his good sense in recognizing his need for help, and I would dutifully admit him for a number of days. After he ate well for several days, abstained from alcohol, and received many visits from his A.A. friends, I would feel he was ready to be launched once more into the world and would send him home.

Several times over the past decade, Alan's wife and daughter moved out when he was drinking and back home again when he was sober. They realized that he was inherently a loving person and always gave him a second chance. As the years rolled by, with every additional hospitalization, there were additional problems at home because of his drinking. Although A.A. is a highly respected and successful organization, Alan stopped attending the meetings. Psychiatric help, tranquilizers, medications, vitamins, good diet, and friends all failed to keep him sober.

About four years ago, after yet another bout of alcoholism, as he was about to be discharged, I asked him if we might pray about his drinking problem, and he appeared eager and ready to accept this mode of healing. The prayer took the form of affirming him and convincing him that he was a precious child of God despite his problem. Because he had felt rejected all of his life, an improvement of his feeling of self-worth was just what he needed. He sighed; he wept; and after we hugged, he exclaimed that he had never had anyone pray for him in his life and that he felt that an enormous burden had been lifted from his shoulders.

Alan has not had a drop to drink since then, and his formerly precarious domestic life has been restored to a healthy one. He has been truly transformed. It was only after reaching his spiritual nature that he was successfully able to control his alcohol problem. Treatment confined only to the needs of his mind and body were unsuccessful. One-on-one prayer was the answer for him. This is not to deny the spiritual side of A.A. or its great success over the years. The one-on-one attention, through prayer, of his private physician may have had an advantage in his particular case over A.A., which emphasizes a group approach. At this writing, he has been sober for the longest period of time: over four years. He speaks at some of the local high schools about the dangers of alcohol and attends A.A. regularly.

Easing the Pain of Terminal Cancer

Emma was a seventy-eight-year-old woman dying from cancer. She was in constant pain and had become bedridden in the hospital. Her two daughters and her husband were not only upset but had many unresolved conflicts among themselves that made it doubly difficult for them to communicate. This problem greatly disturbed Emma and aggravated her condition. One day it became apparent that both the patient and her family needed healing and that prayer was the only way that this could be accomplished. The patient, her family, the nurse on duty, and I all joined hands and prayed for a healing for the patient and for all the family members. Several days later the patient died, but in the days preceding, she had reached a more peaceful state of mind and required much less pain medication. A spiritual healing had taken place. The family members, likewise, reached a more peaceful state by reconciling their differences during her final days, and the stresses that had built up between them were relieved.

The above case proves that God hears our prayers. When a physical healing does not occur, we often cry out that God has failed to answer our prayers. This apparent neglect is difficult for us to understand, but ours is a mysterious Lord, and we must remember that no prayer is not heard by God. His response may be a spiritual healing that has widespread benefits to many family members rather than a physical healing that centers only on the patient. Other benefits may be an energetic pursuit for a cure of the disease or a heightened sense of community responsibility to help others with a similar afflic-tion. This sense of community responsibility may take the form of personal involvement with financial aid to organizations dedicated to fighting that illness.

Heart Attack Survivor

George is a fifty-year-old man who was recently admitted to the Coronary Care Unit (CCU) for a heart attack. He was anxious, had a rapid heart rate, and was suffering from severe chest pain. The essential medical treatment had been begun, but he was still very frightened. I felt he was open to prayer and placed my hand on his chest, thanking the Lord for being present at this time and reassuring George that the Lord was going to enter into his total healing. Almost instantly he sighed deeply and settled back in bed. I could almost see the level of adrenaline in his blood fall as he became more at peace. In addition, the bedside monitor showed his heart rate fall from 110 beats per minute down to 85 beats per minute within a very short time after ending the prayer. This positive effect was accomplished without the aid of any drugs, many of which we know can have multiple side effects. George subsequently had an uncomplicated stay in the hospital and was discharged six days later.

Medically speaking, the greatest enemy to the recent heart attack victim is a fast heart rate. The central area of the heart sustains irreversible damage (necrosis) that eventually heals as a scar. The heart fibers responsible for contracting the heart are replaced by this scar. There is, however, around the center of the dead tissue a peripheral area that sustains damage that is potentially reversible. Fast heart rates, frequently caused or aggravated by fear and anxiety, will cause the area of damage to spread, with a resulting larger, noncontracting scar and a greater chance of becoming a permanent cardiac cripple. The larger the mass of scar tissue, the less effective the heart will be.

A number of drugs such as digitalis, beta-blockers, and excessive sedation can slow a fast heart rate, but they all have side effects. For example, beta-blockers may aggravate lung conditions and heart failure. Anxiety and fear result in an oversecretion of adrenaline and adrenal gland hormones that can lead to frequent palpitations or potentially dangerous rhythm disturbances in addition to the fast heart rate. In recent years, more attention has been focused on the role of emotions, such as stress and anxiety, and the central nervous system in causing lethal cardiac rhythm disturbances.

When these stressful conditions can be ameliorated by calling upon God's healing power and love and peace, what a miracle it is! The Holy Spirit enters into healing as the Comforter and this is very powerful medicine.

Unfortunately, most cardiac patients have had poor health habits for many years. Much attention has been correctly focused upon lowering the amount of fat in the diet, and overall this has been very successful. There are other behavioral factors that cause medical problems such as stress, tobacco abuse, and the lack of regular aerobic exercise. These are very important considerations and need more attention. One of the important things about being a spiritual friend as well as a physician is that patients comply more readily in matters of improving cardiovascular life-style habits. Believe it or not, I've had more than one patient switch from a bad habit to a good one (from smoking to walking), painful as it was, and remark, "I just didn't want to let you down."

Prayer for a Coma Patient

An elderly woman, Irene, had a massive heart attack while driving her car on the highway. On the way to the hospital Emergency Room (ER), she had a cardiac arrest, became comatose, and required a cardiac pacemaker. After a few days in the Intensive Care Unit (ICU), with no sign of awakening from the comatose state, the nurse asked, "Should we write a no-code order?" (This term means no heroic resuscitation.) Her family consisted of two children; one had flown in from the Midwest and the other lived in a nearby town.

That evening, using discernment, it occurred to me that perhaps we all should pray for this woman because the situation looked terribly desperate, and she was not responding satisfactorily to the usual medical treatment. Her cardiac condition seemed to have stabilized but her coma had persisted. The family was most eager to do this, so we went into the patient's room and drew the curtains in order to be private with our prayer. A pulmonary technician was already there, and we asked him if he would like to pray with us, and he said he would. We all placed our hands on Irene and asked the Holy Spirit to come in and do his wondrous works to help to heal her right then. Much to our joy, Irene moved at the conclusion of the prayer, opened her eyes, and actually made attempts to sit up in bed. Her son fell to his knees and prayed and wept. There was so much commotion that the nurse ran in. Her eyes bulged when she saw Irene looking at her and trying to speak. The intern and medical resident were also amazed and promptly asked what had happened. When I told them that we had all just finished praying for her, they just looked stunned, and one said that he had never heard a physician say that before.

The miracle of this healing was that the patient had twelve hours of conversation, which served to be a great blessing to her family. At the end of about twelve hours, her heart finally gave out. We were unable to sustain blood pressure, and she died. Many weeks later, I received a letter from her son (who turned out to be a lawyer) expressing his gratitude for allowing him to pray for his mother and stating how much the prayer meant to him and his sister. This temporary recovery was another example of a healing, though only a transient one, brought about by the power of the Holy Spirit.

The above true cases are representative of hospitalized patients. Two of them died physically, but both were spiritually healed and those around them were as well. A physical cure was not expected in our prayer of healing for Emma, who had terminal cancer, or Irene, who was in coma from a severe heart attack. The Lord answered both prayers in his way. Alan, the alcoholic, and George, who had a heart attack, did survive. Both have been fine patients and are leading productive lives. I often pray a prayer of thanksgiving for their wholeness during the follow-up office visits with each of them.

Whether during office visits or among friends or acquaintances, I frequently see broken hearts, anxieties, fear, and insecurities. When used with discernment, prayer has had unbelievable power in bringing our Lord's peace to these troubled souls. We must remember the Lord loves each of us. We are all children of God regardless of our religious tradition.

A Reconciliation

Frank, an eighty-year-old retired banker, was another patient of mine. He had been an acolyte in the Roman Catholic Church as a young man and had been raised in a very devout Catholic family. In fact, one of his brothers was a priest and two of his sisters were nuns. For reasons best known to him, he had left the church about forty years previously. He had been my patient for about fifteen years. Frank developed cancer of the stomach and also suffered from emphysema, having been a heavy cigarette smoker for many years. He elected not to have surgery or chemotherapy. This request was reluctantly accepted by my colleagues and me. Nevertheless, the subject was never brought up for serious consideration again. Over the ensuing months, his appetite began to decrease progressively and his weight started to fall. Soon he became housebound, and I began regular weekly visits to his home. He required oxygen before too long and needed a host of various medications for his bothersome and persistent coughing. As the weeks went by, he became more anxious as death seemed to be approaching. One day, led by the Holy Spirit, I discerned that he would be open to prayer. To my surprise, he welcomed it. We prayed about a healing relationship for him with God and prayed for an openness to let God back into his life.

Years ago, his parents had become upset that he was not going into the priesthood. One of his sisters had written regularly to him trying, among other things, to bring him back to the church. Following our first effort at praying together, he sighed deeply and began to weep (as did I). This resulted in a peace about him that I had not seen before. The weeks went on, and slowly but surely he became progressively weaker. He rejected several attempts I made to bring a member of the clergy, but he still looked forward to our praying together. He could now talk about the Lord and how he knew he was letting himself be held by the Lord's grace. His dying process was a testimony of God's love for all of his children. His anxiety became less of a problem and he became more at peace at the end. When it became apparent that he would die soon, he asked if we could pray that he might live until the following Monday when his sister would be coming for a visit. God heard our prayers and his sister arrived on the appointed Monday. He wanted to live to see his sister once more. I do not know what transpired between them. He died peacefully the following day. And, as was the case many times before when longtime patients and friends have died, part of me died with him.

There are miracles in this story. Frank was healed and returned to the Lord after many years, and his family was reconciled. I am sure the Lord eased him gently over the bridge from this life to the next. As strange as it may sound, his illness was a miracle, a transformation. He moved from rebellion to reconciliation and the peace that comes from it.

From scripture we learn,

. . . and people brought to him all who were ill with various diseases, . . . and he healed them.

Matthew 4.24

Laying on of Hands

Christian healing often is accompanied by the laying on of hands. As mentioned, touch has a healing power in its own right. Through the laying on of hands we become more visible and perhaps more effective as channels for God's healing love and grace. In this way, we not only demonstrate our own love for the person, but we also allow God's love to penetrate that person's mind, body, and spirit with the greater healing power of the Holy Spirit. There are many examples of ministering with laying on of hands. At a Franciscan retreat, one of the retreatants was suffering from severe pain in her hip. She couldn't walk without the use of a cane. During the healing service, her husband touched her hip and the remainder of us placed our hands on her head and prayed for a healing. She said that she could feel the heat rushing to the hip area. The pain disappeared and she spent the rest of our active weekend without the cane. Her hip is still relatively pain-free at this writing, three years later.

A Case of Instant Physical Healing

Mary is a seventy-year-old woman who fell and fractured her wrist. She was suffering from a dropped wrist as a result of nerve damage caused by the fracture, and was unable to use the wrist in a normal fashion. Nerve stimulation studies confirmed the damage, and she was scheduled for hand and wrist surgery for a Tuesday months later. The night before surgery she called her prayer group and asked for an all-night prayer vigil for a healing. Tuesday morning her wrist drop had disappeared, and surgery was canceled. She had suffered from this condition for several months before the day of the scheduled surgery. The surgeon couldn't believe it and called me on the phone. He had never seen anything like this before.

Healings as instantaneous as this one have rarely been my experience. The exceptional cases of instant healing have occurred at healing services sponsored by churches, where perhaps thirty or more people experience the laying on of hands and prayer for their individual needs. Very often there will be several individuals that have a healing at that service. Most often, however, the healing makes progress at slower rates. A series of prayer sessions may have to be carried out over a period of weeks or months. As mentioned earlier, physical healings sometimes don't occur at all, but prayer is answered. In certain instances, the patient may have an inner healing of a longstanding hurt, a healing of anxiety, a reconciliation, a call to discipleship, a lifting of depression, or an awareness of latent gifts not previously recognized that God may wish to be used for his glory. We must constantly remind ourselves that what we ask God to give us may not be what he has in mind for us.

Praise, Thanksgiving, and Affirmation

Everyone relishes praise; it is a sign of approval and support. Our Lord also loves our praise. The Psalms are filled with lines of praise. It is our duty to praise God just for giving us life in addition to acknowledging the many gifts and blessings he has given us. Many writers feel our prayers should start with praise and thanksgiving. I don't know whether there is an official "order of events," but it seems that praise and thanksgiving should be part of our prayers. We should not restrict our prayers to requests only.

A prayer of affirmation is frequently used in Christian healing. It is thanking God for the healing that he is already bringing about. It is a prayer of joyous expectancy, a prayer of faith, one that presumes complete healing before it has had time to materialize. We expect healing, but the one that God chooses; we trust in God's plan rather than our own hopes or expectations. Thanksgiving follows affirmation as we thank God for his commencement of the healing process. Hence, thanksgiving presupposes acceptance of God's healing grace. The power of affirmation is described in scripture. "Therefore I tell you, whatever you ask for in prayer, believe that you have received it, and it will be yours" (Mark 11.24). "And I will do whatever you ask in my name, so that the Son may bring glory to the Father. You may ask me for anything in my name, and I will do it" (John 14.13–14).

5

A Vehicle for God's Love and Inner Healing

The Lord Is Always There

We are called as Christians to be reconcilers to the world around us much as Christ was called to reconcile us to God. Even small things like a phone call, a letter, a visit, or a gift may have a lasting impact on someone's spiritual journey. The Lord is present in all the situations of our life although he is not always recognized. His presence is expressed through people that drop into our life or through events, pleasant or unpleasant, that allow him to open our hearts. People and circumstances are frequently interposed in our path as a means for him to speak to us, to affirm us. It is all part of his plan for each of us, a plan that re-creates and transforms us over and over again as we become more Christlike.

No matter what our vocation is, we all have ample opportunities to be vehicles for God's love and inner healing. A teacher hugging a child and wiping away its tears has the same opportunity to be a channel of God's love as a health-care provider in a hospital.

I hope to show, through these cases chosen at random, the power of the Holy Spirit at work in my particular profession. I believe that it is our responsibility as Christians to share our victories with others and thereby offer encouragement and hope. We should be witnesses to God's grace in our own lives and tell others what happens when the Lord's healing power enters into the lives of our patients. When a healing occurs it needs to be shared! This decaying world needs these victories in order to uplift each of us. We must proclaim in a world of evil, "God is good." Permit me to share with you some of the wonders of his goodness that I have witnessed firsthand.

No Longer Alone

Lorraine, a sixty-five-year-old woman, was frightened and felt abandoned because she was living alone during the holidays. After listening to her deeply felt concerns I asked her, though she was Jewish, if we could pray about all of this. She said she didn't know how to pray. We sat down in the office that day, held hands, and began to pray. The prayer consisted mainly of our giving thanks to our common Father for entering her heart and giving her inner peace and love. At the conclusion of our prayer, she sighed, wept, and displayed a new inner peace. We then walked arm-in-arm down the hall. She no longer felt alone; here was someone who cared. Lorraine has since been reaching out to help others, which has given a new dimension and joy to her life. She makes a special effort during holidays, which are happy times for many people, but can also be the loneliest days of the year for others. Mother Teresa said, "For the worst disease in the world is not leprosy or tuberculosis but the feeling of being unwanted, unloved, and abandoned by everyone."[1]

Spiritual Friends

Rob, a retired milkman, drives up from Delaware for a blood pressure and diabetes check about every four months.

---

[1] Mother Teresa of Calcutta, *The Love of Christ: Spiritual Counsels*, Georges Gorrée and Jean Barbier, eds. (San Francisco: Harper and Row, 1982), 26–27.

We both eagerly await the visit as we have learned that our visit will end with prayers for each other and thanks to God for looking after each of us. We have more than a doctor-patient relationship; we are spiritual friends. He often will say at the very beginning of the visit, "Don't forget, before I leave we have to pray together." We catch up with each other to see what God has been doing with our lives. Have our prayers been answered? Are more prayers needed for a special situation? Have there been some unexpected blessings that we can rejoice about? Any small victories? No matter what the prayer agenda is, by the end of each visit we both feel uplifted and reassured of God's never-ending presence and help. Our Lord's response often comes in unexpected and strange ways and comes at his pace, not ours.

Successful Surgery

Mark, an executive from a car dealership, drives fifty miles to have me check his heart and blood pressure. He postponed knee surgery until we could pray a prayer of affirmation together, thanking God for the healing we knew he would bring about after surgery. Following successful surgery, we said a prayer of thanksgiving. We now pray for each other's needs routinely with each visit. Mark has started up a prayer group and has been taking courses in scripture at a local college. The Lord seems to be leading him slowly into the ministry.

Day by day, the story grows, the miracles continue, and the power and love of our Father manifests itself. As we pray together, share our lives and our victories, and affirm one another, we develop an inner knowledge of his presence, which works itself into everything we do.

A Struggle with Uncontrolled Diabetes

Tom, a fifty-three-year-old man, arrived in the ER with a barely palpable, very low blood pressure and a fever of 102°. He had been diagnosed a diabetic about twenty years previously and had suffered two heart attacks in the past, one in his mid-thirties and one in his late forties. He had not taken good care of himself over the years with some tobacco and alcohol abuse, was overweight, and did not take his diabetes medication regularly. Soon after his arrival at the hospital, Tom was diagnosed as having septicemia (a bloodstream infection) emanating from a severely infected foot. His hospital stay was complicated and prolonged, lasting several weeks. During the course of his stay, he had heart failure, liver coma, anemia, and kidney failure requiring dialysis. He suffered ventricular tachycardia (a lethal cardiac rhythm disturbance requiring special treatment), another heart attack, and then a bone infection and gangrene of the foot, which required amputation below the knee. He also had a large amount of water in his lungs along with evidence of pneumonia. Because of all of these events, his diabetes had gone out of control, which, in turn, complicated his other conditions.

During those initial days, we all prayed for a healing. Tom slipped into a coma soon after his arrival at the hospital. Friends, clergy, and relatives all were involved in asking God for a miracle. With the aid of prayers and all the best care that the physicians, nurses, and technicians could bring to bear, he awoke after several days from the coma and after a number of weeks was discharged from the hospital. A few weeks after his discharge, I waited with great anticipation for his follow-up office visit. The day arrived. My eyes filled with tears as I watched this man slowly struggle down the hall with crutches. As I walked halfway up the hall to meet him, we both must have sensed the miracle of it all. We said nothing and embraced, tears flowing down from our eyes. We thanked God for the victory, each in our own way.

Amazing Contrast

I subsequently mentioned this case at a church gathering where I was presenting the medical consequences of a nuclear explosion. The amazing contrast was clear for all to see. Here on the one hand, was the great amount of human effort in the form of scientific and prayer energy spent over many weeks to save this one precious soul (as in Tom's case), and on the other hand, the loss of unknown millions of human lives in a matter of minutes from a nuclear war. We must all pray for the Lord to come into the hearts of world leaders. There is a real horse race going on; it is neck and neck, and the finishing post is around the bend. The race is between nuclear disaster and the Holy Spirit lighting up the hearts of people around the world to demand peaceful coexistence. Let us all constantly pray for God's victory. There is no alternative.

That church gathering was in 1987. Since then, the world finds itself confronting two serious and growing problems: the AIDS epidemic and illegal drugs and the crime, violence, and addiction that accompany drugs. Prayers the world over have resulted in an easing of East-West tensions, but now, once again, our Lord's guidance and grace must be brought into play.

We must pray for the AIDS patients—all the ones I have treated died at a very young age. At this writing, my state of residence, New Jersey, ranks fourth in the nation, with nearly 6,000 AIDS cases. Between 70,000 and 105,000 people are infected with HIV in New Jersey alone![2] The overwhelming majority die within two years, although medications are being rapidly developed to lengthen the lives of those infected.

It is estimated that the accumulated medical costs for AIDS nationwide will be $3.5 billion by the end of 1989 and $7.5 billion by 1992.[3] Aside from the human tragedy, we have also this great financial burden. Who is to pay for all of this? The cost in terms of loss of life, suffering, and the economy is truly mind-boggling. AIDS is the most serious epidemic in modern times. We must all pray that an effective cure or vaccine will soon be found.

We must also pray that the easing of East-West tensions will enable us to divert a large amount of money from the production of nuclear weapons to remedying the pressing social problems of today: the squalor and hopelessness of the inner cities, the high crime rate, the subhuman conditions in our jails, the increasing number of homeless, and the sorry state of education. These problems demand an answer.

We must pray for the young children of the inner city ghettos, who, devoid of hope and love, are led to drug dealing, often by peer groups or single parents who can't make ends meet. The acquisition of enormous amounts of money from drug dealing leads to both gang wars and more crime.

---

[2] Molley Joel Coye, *AIDS: A Report on the HIV Epidemic in New Jersey*, State of New Jersey Department of Health (Fall 1989), Executive Summary i.

[3] Ibid., ii.

C. S. Lewis describes the need to reach out to others:

> It may be possible for each to think too much of his own potential glory hereafter; it is hardly possible for him to think too often or too deeply about that of his neighbor.[4]

He goes on to say,

> Next to the Blessed Sacrament itself, your neighbor is the holiest object presented to your senses.[5]

By meditating on these words, let us pray that our hearts may be softened and our minds opened to God's guidance. He will show each of us how we may use our own gifts to find solutions to the world's problems if we but listen to him.

Balloons

Henry was a fifty-year-old insurance salesman who had been diagnosed as having bacterial endocarditis (an infection of the heart valves). Fortunately no significant damage to his heart valves occurred because he was unusually fortunate to have had very early treatment for his condition. The most difficult part of his treatment was that he needed intravenous penicillin for several weeks, first in the hospital and then at home.

Henry had made "hundreds" of complaints, including sore veins, black and blue arms from many blood tests, poor appetite, sore joints, no sleep, cranky nurses, and concern about his job. He was tired of the whole medical establishment. Despite his complaints, I really liked him, as I knew him to be a caring man with a good sense of humor. At last the treatments were over! In order to make this a grand celebration, the Holy Spirit told me to send a dozen balloons to Henry's home with happy messages on each one, such as, "Congratulations," "Happy Birthday," "It's a boy," etc.—a mélange of sayings. What fun! He almost cried on the phone with joy. He had never heard of a "crazy thing like that being done" by a patient's physician. I had never heard of that before either, but I feel that God has a

---

[4] C. S. Lewis, *The Weight of Glory and Other Addresses* (New York: Macmillan, 1949), 18.
[5] Ibid., 19.

sense of humor and enjoys springing surprises as much as anyone, so I'm sure that he, too, enjoyed the fun of the balloons. Many months later, Henry and I still have a chuckle over this.

Understanding Parents

John was the typical all-American student at one of the local universities. While in his dorm, he suddenly clutched his chest and fell over on the floor and stopped breathing. Perhaps ten minutes passed before proper CPR was administered. When he arrived at the hospital, and I saw him for the first time, he was unresponsive; his cardiogram showed ventricular fibrillation (a fast lethal rhythm). His heart was electrically shocked immediately upon arrival and this treatment successfully terminated the lethal rhythm disturbance. Simultaneously, he was placed on a ventilator because he was not breathing. Both of his parents were physicians living in Michigan. For several weeks, his progress was closely followed in a special unit. John never recovered consciousness. Before meeting the parents I prayed that the Lord let a peaceful and understanding relationship develop because not only would they be understandably upset, but they might also be overly demanding and critical, as they were both physicians.

They were wonderful. They were understanding and co-operative in every way. After many weeks and many consultations with neurologists, it was apparent that John was brain dead. Together with the hospital chaplain, we all prayed silently and held hands as the series of tests to prove brain death were carried out. The tests confirmed brain death and this handsome child died. His organs were donated to others, thus giving other people in need of them a second chance.

The enormous amount of energy these brain death cases take out of a physician cannot be overestimated. The stress is incalculable! When physicians have this much stress at work year in and year out, they have a great need for quiet, reflection, restoration, and a sense of peace daily at home in order to maintain any sense of composure.

We, as physicians, are often so involved in every way with our patients, that we lose sight of the fact that all people will die at some time. Some patients will die no matter what the physician does. We physicians suffer a sense of failure to some extent when we lose a patient. As I said before, for many of us, some part of us is lost with each patient that we lose.

This loss is draining and can lead to exhaustion. Hence, there is a need for prayer, a need for turning all stress over to God and then simply doing the best we can. Paul said we should pray unceasingly. Praying unceasingly takes practice. But, with persistence, one can subconsciously pray—the word *Jesus*, for example—even during the busiest time of the day. Eventually praying this way may encompass 20 percent of your working hours, and, as time goes on, it is possible for praying to become a habit almost 100 percent of the time, although I realize this is a difficult goal when there are so many unexpected, distracting, and time-consuming events happening every day. St. Francis's prayer was "My God and my all." He learned to pray in this manner constantly so that it became a habit. It was a prayer of constant praise and thanksgiving.

Need of a Hug

Joe is a seventy-year-old retired man who was recovering from recent surgery for cancer of the colon. In addition, he was being treated for cancer of the prostate and had bone metastasis (spread of cancer to the bones) that was discovered about one year before the colon cancer. I had known him for many years as a patient and helped him through a heart attack years before.

One day Joe called our office nurse stating that he had abdominal pain and didn't know where to go for help as his gastroenterologist said he needed to see me first, and the urologist and general surgeon were not available. He was frightened and felt alone. It would have been easy for anyone in his position to feel abandoned or rejected by those who so recently had helped him. The office nurse told him to come down right away; no appointment was necessary. He soon arrived, his eyes full of tears as he explained how rejected he felt and how appreciative he was to be seen immediately. After examining him, I realized that he had nothing serious, just a bad case of indigestion. I gave him a routine blood test and wrote a prescription. Sensing all the many fears he was experiencing, we stood still for a moment and then hugged. He broke out in tears as he walked down the hall.

The next day his wife called to say that he was feeling better and that what he really needed most of all was the hug that we had shared. Because of this hug, he knew he was not forgotten and that someone cared. A hug does say a lot, doesn't it? Words need not be spoken. A hug may signify everything from joy at a party to compassion in the workplace.

The "Seizure Patient" and the "Besieged" Physician

We are all creatures of habit. We like our little daily routines that appear to give us peace and security. On the other hand, these daily rituals can rule our lives. The problem with living in such a habitual way is that we may be unwilling to be open to new challenges and opportunities. A change or a break in familiar routines may cause stress and discomfort and can be disquieting and make us insecure. Because of this discomfort, it is tempting to shy away from any change at all. Therefore, we often have difficulty in handling surprises, especially when they are unpleasant. Even if I have only a minute or so in which to respond, in recent years I have found that praying in silence during the decision-making process can be of immense help. Turning the problem immediately over to God and letting him work through me has had amazing success. The following case is an example.

I arrived on the medical floor of the hospital one weekday morning and was greeted by several nurses, the night shift going off and the day shift about to start. They were concerned about Helen, a forty-year-old patient, who had been disturbing everyone all night by crying out, shouting, jumping out of bed, lying on the floor, and even banging her head on the floor. She was also being abusive to the nursing staff and house officers. She had been given a sedative for agitation without effect. I had known Helen for a long time. She had survived many years of torment as she struggled with both alcohol and drug abuse. She seemed in recent years to be doing much better. We had even prayed together in the office from time to time giving thanks for all the good things that recently were happening in her life, such as going on to further education and becoming a vital member of her church. For me she truly had become a living example of God's grace.

On this morning, she was apparently suffering a migraine attack. I prayed for the Spirit to speak through me as I hurried down to her room. The nursing supervisor as well as a large number of patients were all watching to see the fireworks. I felt that I was in the spotlight and besieged by everyone on the floor to "do something," not only to correct the condition immediately but to do so to everyone's satisfaction, including the patient, nursing staff, patients on the floor, hospital administration, and me. After I helped her back to bed and held her hand, we prayed together for God to come into her heart and give her his peace and love. As I stayed with her for several moments, I could see her become more relaxed and peaceful. She eventually quieted down and fell off to sleep. Helen was a model patient for the remaining three days of her hospital stay. Her "seizure" was largely due to the migraine attack accompanied by agitation and hyperventilation. The Lord brought her peace using me as a vehicle of caring. When the others asked me what happened, I smiled and said, "We prayed together," and slowly walked away.

There are two concepts demonstrated in this case: the power of prayer to heal when used for one who is open to a healing and the power of prayer to help the healer take the necessary action. Helen was open to prayer, and I discerned this. She was healed almost immediately and remained peaceful for the rest of her hospital stay. I knew what to do to calm Helen, though I hadn't planned anything. I opened my mind and heart to the Holy Spirit, and he led me to choose the words that would soothe and comfort most. The Holy Spirit will guide our words and our actions as long as we remain open to this source of power.

Whenever an individual prays with another, a great amount of love is expressed. One who prays must care enough to take time to be present, to frequently lay hands on the other person, and to ask God to use him or her as a channel of healing. This is love in action. When the prayer is direct, to the point, and asks God's help for a specific condition or illness, this is what I call a prayer of intercession. At times, a prayer of affirmation may be even stronger and more powerful, since we are thanking God for his healing already underway. An affirmation prayer is a prayer of faith. Regardless of the prayer used, there is a bond, a special connection, between the people involved. Praying with someone has a healing quality greater than praying for someone. It develops an authentic spiritual relationship. In my view, it is more powerful than saying, "I'll pray for you in church" or "I'll have my prayer group put your name on our list."

From Death to Discipleship

Harold is a sixty-two-year-old man who died transiently in the CCU when his heart went into a lethal ventricular fibrillation during the first few hours after a heart attack but was brought back from cardiac arrest by defibrillation (electric shock). Aside from a couple of minor complications due to his heart attack itself, he had a rather smooth hospital course and was eventually discharged. Shortly after his cardiac arrest, but while still in the hospital, however, we prayed together, thanking God for already starting his healing process. His anxiety and fear of further episodes of cardiac arrest and electric shocks seemed to be relieved as he was able to relax a bit and trust in God's grace. Less anxiety usually results in less heart palpitations.

Recently, while rejoicing about his recovery during an office visit, Harold mentioned for the first time how much our praying together had meant to him and let me know about the peace of mind it had given him. He went on to say that during his hospital stay, one of the hospital volunteers had come to his bedside within hours after his transient death. She was in great distress and said that she had heard he had been brought back from death and that she wanted to talk to him. He noted she seemed desperate and on the verge of tears, and he asked her why. Her husband had just had a similar heart attack but did not survive. He did not come back. She desperately needed to talk to someone who had survived a similar event, and she felt a bond with this unknown man who had experienced death and was her husband's approximate age. Was he at peace during those brief moments before he was resuscitated? Harold then went on to relate how he listened to this distressed woman as she poured out her grief upon him. He asked her to pull the curtains and asked if he could pray for her and her deceased husband. He had never prayed for anyone before, but since he had seen God's power come into his own life through prayer, he felt he could do the same for this troubled woman. After he listened further to her story and prayed for her, the woman sighed and quietly wept. Shortly thereafter, Harold noted the woman's face was transformed from one of desperation and anguish to one of peace, as she pulled open the curtains and left his room. We both marveled at the power of the Holy Spirit first to heal him and then, while still a patient in the CCU, to enable him to be a vehicle of healing by sharing the heavy burden of the troubled volunteer. What a powerful witness to God's love! This story shows a man's transition from death to discipleship.

"Heal me, O Lord, and I will be healed . . ."

Anna, a sixty-year-old secretary, arrived at my office complaining of a fever and cough she had had for several days. She also had noticed a persistent rash on her legs for many months. Various skin lotions failed to improve the rash. She was short of breath as she related her symptoms and her face, lips and fingernail beds appeared cyanotic (bluishness caused by lack of oxygen). She had undergone hip replacement surgery for her severely arthritic hip, requiring blood transfusions at a time prior to knowledge about the AIDS epidemic. Since routine blood screening for AIDS didn't start until about 1983, she had always wondered since then if she had received any contaminated blood, though she had never mentioned it to me. Up to now, she had refused to accept the idea. She was admitted to the hospital, and it was clear she was suffering from pneumonia.

Despite treatment, her condition deteriorated day by day. Suspecting AIDS-related pneumonia, which was subsequently diagnosed by specific tests, I instituted intravenous antibiotics for this condition. Despite this treatment, her condition continued to deteriorate. She was transferred to the ICU. Though a ventilator to assist her breathing was necessary, she refused it and desired to be a "no-code," that is, no elaborate resuscitation, no ventilator. At this point she had been told her diagnosis, and she knew the prognosis. She stated that she would rather die than be placed on artificial ventilation. She was then given an oxygen mask that had to be strapped to her face to allow oxygen to be delivered more efficiently to her lungs. The more Anna struggled with the mask, the more oxygen she used up unnecessarily and the more cyanotic she became. Her struggles resulted in using up the little oxygen that remained for her bodily needs. Sedation could not be used as this would only depress her respiration further. Could we keep her alive long enough for the antibiotics to take effect?

At this crucial point in time, there were three of us beside the struggling patient: an ICU nurse, a pulmonary technician, and me. The pulmonary technician had always impressed me as a sensitive, caring, spiritual woman. I noted for the first time that the nurse's name tag had a dove (a symbol of the Holy Spirit) attached to it. I asked the patient if she would allow us to pray for her and she nodded her head. We all placed our hands upon her. Acting as channels for God's healing, we prayed for God's inner peace to take control, allowing her to stop her excessive struggling. We remained for some time in the room with her. After several minutes, she appeared more relaxed and at peace. This was a critical point. It would be several hours before the medicine could take hold. At the same time, she was on the verge of dying from respiratory failure. Over the next few hours her blood gases started to improve as did her color. A few days later, her fever left her, and she was gradually weaned off the mask and sent to the medical floor. Not too long afterwards, her appetite and strength started to return. The antibiotics had worked and she was able to be discharged without any symptoms. When I saw Anna in the office one week later, she looked as well as she had before the pneumonia. The Lord answered our prayers and saved her from her distress.

> I sought the Lord, and he
> answered me;
> he delivered me from my
> fears.

Those who look to him are radiant;
their faces are never covered with
shame.
This poor man called, and the Lord
heard him;
he saved him out of all his
troubles.

Psalm 34.4–6

We who were in the ICU room with Anna during that crucial time felt that it was God's grace that allowed her to let go and trust that all would be well. Although she continues to do well, she still carries the virus. We are all praying that a cure will be found in the near future. Her personal religious tradition is unknown to me, if, indeed, she practices one at all. She remembers our prayers and appreciates the outcome. But for those of us who prayed for her, we rejoice in the power of God's healing, which serves as a reaffirmation of our own faith. This, by itself, is priceless and more than enough. We glorify the Lord who saves us.

. . . and call upon me in the day of
trouble;
I will deliver you, and you will
honor me.

Psalm 50.15

Heal me, O Lord, and I will be
healed;
save me and I will be saved,
for you are the one I praise.

Jeremiah 17.14

A Sunday Afternoon Phone Call

The phone rang in my house on a Sunday afternoon. I was off duty for the weekend and felt somewhat put upon for having to talk to a patient on my day off. The patient, Joanne, said that she was sorry for disturbing me but that she was worried about what a nurse had said in the ICU just before her husband died six months earlier. I rapidly tried to reconstruct as many of the details as I could while she talked. The story slowly came back to me. Joanne's husband had suffered from an advanced case of cirrhosis of the liver with intestinal bleeding spells. He arrived at the hospital in a stuporous state. At some point he vomited and some of the vomitus seeped into his lungs causing a dreadful pneumonia that was complicated by liver failure. He was placed on a ventilator to enable him to breathe. Despite heroic efforts, he eventually died from a combination of these factors. The nurse mentioned that if he had reported his illness perhaps a week or so earlier the outcome might have been different. The widow felt guilty for not having forced her unwilling spouse to seek medical help earlier. This guilt had been gnawing at her for the past six months.

I listened to Joanne's story as she expressed her feelings of pain and guilt that Sunday on the phone. These hurts caused her such intense grief and misery that she felt she could not get on with her life without bringing them out in the open and discussing them.

As I listened, I prayed that the Holy Spirit, the Comforter, would speak through me in a clear and loving way. After I assured her that she had done absolutely everything she could have done and remarked that she had always been a loving wife, I heard her sigh, her voice quivering on the edge of crying, and she said, "Thanks so much." We both received a blessing from this conversation. Despite my usual dislike of receiving professional calls when off duty, I thanked God for this call. Joanne was now able to move on with her life, having successfully been able to expel this burden of guilt that had been smothering her for the past several months.

Phone calls like this one can wind up being a blessing; many times they make a big difference in a patient's life. In situations like this it is miraculous how easily a complicated problem can be solved and how quickly the troubled caller can be healed when we ask God to speak through us. On more than one occasion, I have found actual praying on the phone with a patient to be an immeasurable help. Not surprisingly, we both receive a blessing even from this form of communication. How important inner peace is for each of us. When an opportunity appears whereby we can be a channel for peace to another, what joy this can bring. This is what Christianity is all about—the priceless pearl of God's inner peace. John Wesley stated it so well in one of his sermons:

> What Christianity promises is accomplished in our souls. It becomes a completion of all the inward principles promised in the gospels. It is holiness and happiness, the image of God impressed upon our spirits. It is a fountain of peace and love springing up to everlasting life.[6]

Despite the success of many of my phone conversations with patients, phone calls can also be a problem. At the end of a long, tedious day, to be faced with a host of calls to return can be the last straw. Nevertheless, it is best to answer each call, in order to start the next day with a clean slate. I have to continually remind myself that though the questions and concerns may seem trivial to me, they are often very important to each patient.

Today I have fewer after-hours phone calls than there were twenty years ago. Almost without exception, when I'm called to get up to meet someone late at night or in the early morning hours at the ER, the patients are ill enough to require hospitalization.

Some phone calls after hours have been humorous. One woman worried about the ivy that was climbing from the ground to her second floor balcony. She was afraid she might contract an illness from it because a dog frequently watered it. I once received a call from a patient in a restaurant: Should she use French or Russian dressing on the salad—which would settle best? She had to know because the waiter was about to take the order. A first generation Italian-American woman called to complain that her husband was "eating too much

---

[6] John Wesley, *The Holy Spirit and Power*, paraphrased by Clare Weekby (Plainfield, NJ: Logos International, 1977), 173.

jungle food." I pictured him eating bananas, which I never found to be particularly harmful. After further questioning, I realized she was referring to "junk food."

Many anxious calls can be handled with simple reassurance. But if the call results in some doubt about the diagnosis, it is better to see the problem firsthand, as you will only worry about it all night. In the cases where I took care of the problem personally, I found I could go back to bed and sleep better (and so did the patient).

I feel a few words must be said on behalf of clergy and practicing physicians regarding nonemergency phone calls. In our service-oriented professions, we cannot be available all the time. I feel it is more of an emergency for a healer to be alone with God and his family or friends than it is for him or her to answer foolish phone calls, especially after hours. A healer must have adequate backup (colleagues taking turns being on call) in order to avoid burnout. (I will be discussing burnout in chapter 6.) Also, the healer should not interfere with the independence and decision-making process of a person by giving a rubber-stamp "OK" to all decisions no matter how small, even if the patient thinks he or she needs it. Healers, in order to live longer and be more effective, may have to learn to withdraw to places of solitude and peace more frequently as society's problems and demands continue to grow. As Paul said, "Let us not be weary in well doing: for in due season we shall reap, if we faint not" (Galatians 6.9). We can accomplish great good if we don't work ourselves to the point of nervous breakdown. Remember the proviso, "if we faint not."

House Calls

While it is true that house calls are not as routinely done now as in the past, they are still done on occasion, especially for those who are housebound. More than once, I've been surprised by a patient who reminded me of a house call I had made many years before to visit an aging mother or other family member. The family had always remembered this, though I had long ago forgotten it. I remember the relief I felt when I saw the pediatrician's car roll into the driveway when one of my children was five years old and had a 105° fever. I was at the receiving end, for a change, and have never forgotten how important this was to me.

Physicians make fewer house calls today, partly because of the increased role of diagnostic tests and equipment that cannot leave the office, and partly because of the inconvenience to the busy physician. Despite these difficulties, it is important for the physician to be prepared to make house calls at least for housebound patients. When the physician goes to a patient's home, he or she sees the living conditions and environment of the patient, which can reveal quite a bit about the patient's health. By making a house call, the physician also develops a more personal relationship with the patient that may allow the patient to feel more secure and at ease. House calls may be an inconvenience, but they should not disappear from the medical profession.

Old Friends and Soda Bread

I often made house calls to Kathleen, a recent patient of mine who was a housebound elderly woman with an amputated leg and heart disease. I suppose it was more of a social visit than a professional one, because I saw this dear soul about once a month. I always called her on the phone to let her know I was coming before I left the office for our visits. I always suspected that each time Kathleen sat waiting in her wheelchair in her living room looking out the window for my car, because I had only to knock once, and the door would fly open, and there she would be, smiling as she beckoned me in. As soon as I was inside, she always steered her wheelchair toward the kitchen. We would chat and enjoy some tea and fresh Irish soda bread. Since it was always the end of the day, we could have a thimble of Irish Mist as well.

Occasionally, a friend drove her to my office instead. At those times, she would bring a box of recently baked cookies. Whether she was at home or in the office, during our visits I would unobtrusively check for any shortness of breath, swollen ankles, cough, etc. and would note her energy level. Then I would check her blood pressure, heart, and lungs. We shared many thoughts besides medical ones during our visits. We frequently prayed together about anything that was on her mind. We had become spiritual friends. What a blessing we were to each other. Kathleen passed away at home in her sleep a few months ago. As in the case of the banker, I felt I had lost both a patient and a very special friend.

6

Avoiding Healer Exhaustion

Burnout

We all are constantly bombarded by life's never-ending demands. Aside from the demands of their patients, physicians have unique stresses such as peer review of charts, done by at least three different groups or organizations; pressures from administration to send the hospitalized patient home soon (but not too soon); family pressures to keep the patient in the hospital longer (but not too long or they will run the risk of losing their coverage); an increasing number of forms to fill out; frozen Medicare fees; increasing overhead; and high patient expectations for complete medical and surgical cures. Other serious concerns for the physician are the liability crisis, the need to keep up-to-date in his or her field, the need to spend time with family, and community responsibilities. And, oh yes, he or she must keep in good physical shape and still save time for being quiet and for relaxing as well.

It is easy for any professional person to burn out, given all the demands upon each one of us. This condition can occur in many other job situations as well as in the healing professions. Enormous job tensions are virtually the norm in our society today. This stress can lead to serious health problems and must be addressed in the healing process.

As part of the office visit or physical examination, I ask the patient if he or she has a significant amount of tension at work or at home. An overwhelming majority mention that there is a significant amount of job tension present, and many are carrying personal burdens or tensions related to family as well.

For example, I always repeat the blood pressure reading after I ask the patient to sigh, and, demonstrating a sigh myself, I ask the patient to imagine that he or she is lying on the beach or in a hammock. This activity serves as a mini-meditation. Without fail, the systolic blood pressure will drop at least ten points as the patient becomes much more relaxed. Doesn't this tell us something about the role of tension in each person's life? We are all running about in a state of tension of some degree or another. The nurses in my office now record all blood pressures of patients "after a deep sigh."

One patient of mine, a mother of a busy young family with six children, hides herself in her bedroom closet for half an hour every morning in order to be alone with God. She feels this is the only way she will not be distracted. You can imagine her husband's surprise the first time this happened. He was looking for her before going to work in the morning and finally found her sitting on the floor of the closet with the door closed. After some explanation, he finally accepted this behavior as her way of being quiet before her busy day gets underway. By doing this, she remains calm for the rest of the day. She takes literally what Matthew says in scripture:

> But when you pray, go into your room, close the door and pray to your Father, who is unseen. Then your Father, who sees what is done in secret, will reward you.
>
> Matthew 6.6

We live in a frantic and disconnected society and each of us needs this at-oneness with our Lord.

Leadership Renewal

Do I have a balance in my life? Do I make time for renewal, rest, and family? How can I avoid burnout? The work ethic is part of our society. We may feel guilty if we find spare time to take a nap or simply lounge around and accomplish nothing. Many leaders in business and the professions are driving themselves toward exhaustion or nervous breakdowns as they try to meet endless deadlines under increasing amounts of stress. Although much that is written about stress in the business world in modern society concerns all levels of the work force, we must not forget that leaders of our businesses and organizations need special renewal and prayer. Workers in large corporations have problems that often land on the laps of the executives, who have problems of their own. This is especially true for physicians, who listen to problems all day and try their best to help their patients. So many patients forget that physicians have their own problems. To whom does the physician or clergyman turn? Who heals the healer?

Leadership renewal is, therefore, crucial. Our leaders, men and women in the service professions and executives in large corporations, who every day reach out to help others or make decisions that affect hundreds of employees, must be ministered to but often are not. When there is no adequate relief, the doors for long-term devastation are opened, which can result in dependence on alcohol or drugs and lead to nervous breakdowns, various illnesses, and even suicide. There is no universal prescription for renewal. Each person, therefore, must find his or her own way to reduce stress. No matter how this renewal is accomplished, it is imperative that it is, indeed, accomplished.

Keeping My Head above Water
(What Works for Me)

I have tried various approaches to keeping my own head above water in the midst of a very busy and demanding practice. I've always been interested in how busy people continue to do well despite their hectic pace of living, and I've always been struck by the amount of discipline displayed in their personal lives. A disciplined life can help bring order out of the chaos and help the individual maintain some sense of sanity. In order to be whole, it is necessary to use discipline and to remember to consider the whole person—mind, body, and spirit—in a life-long program. The following method has worked for me, but

you may want to try something different. Through it I attempt
to address what I call our "wholeness"—the whole person.

Scripture

It seems that none of us can read too much scripture. Even
theologians who know a great deal of scripture get new insights
when they reread the Lord's words. As we become more and
more familiar with the Bible through daily readings, the Lord
becomes more a part of our lives and helps us in our daily
decisions. As a layperson, I have found it most helpful to read
a daily missal containing a small passage of scripture and a brief
comment relating it to the present. Currently I am reading
Living with Christ, published by Novalis in Canada. As mentioned above, this is a paperbound booklet issued each month
with lectionary readings and weekday and Sunday liturgy. *The
Word among Us* contains a group of essays and meditations
based on the daily lectionary for every day of the year. William
Barclay's Daily Bible Series offers insightful interpretations and
historical information about the scriptures. It has been difficult
for me to sit down and read straight through the Bible from
Genesis to Revelation. By using the above books, the Bible has
been easier for me to understand and the experience has been
more rewarding. By following the daily scriptures as found in
these books, I have a sense of community with my fellow
believers who are following these same passages during the
different phases of the church year. There is a definite advantage in reading the day's scripture before the Sunday church
service that is using the same liturgy. This practice may reinforce
the scripture's message or may broaden or deepen your understanding of the passage.

Spiritual Journal

I also maintain a daily spiritual journal in which I write
about all my problems, prayers, and questions that I like to talk
to the Lord about, as well as many of my happy moments.

For my spiritual journal I use a book that has the year
printed on the cover such as a diary or appointment book. In it

there is a full page for every day of the year. Each day I write my cares, my prayers, bits of scripture, or other readings that have special meaning to me for that particular day. I list the names of various patients who are ill, and I pray for them on an ongoing basis. I also list the needs of loved ones, needs of my own, and thanksgivings for God's help, successes, healings, and blessings.

My spiritual journal also serves as a testimony to my own spiritual progress over the years. It is enlightening to see how the Lord has been active in my life by reading the thoughts and prayers in my journals from years past. Once in a while I pull out previous years' journals and note what prayers were on my mind then and where I was on my spiritual journey and then relate this to my present situation. Rereading my old journals serves as an affirmation of God's ever-present love and grace because they demonstrate that he is always with me under all circumstances.

I visited Bishop Lance Webb in his home in Florida several years ago, and he pointed out his yearly journals, which spanned about forty years, neatly arranged in chronological order in the bookcase in his study. As Bishop Webb remarks in his book, *Disciples for Life in the Age of Aquarius*:

> These books—one for each year since 1947—reflect the story of my pilgrimage through difficult testings and opportunities that have come to me—the weary burdens I have borne, the triumphant experiences of victory over my phony self-demands, and the equally triumphant experience of sharing with others who were winning the victory of faith. [1]

The chronological order and the resulting accessibility of Bishop Webb's journals, each representing a certain time in his spiritual development, greatly impressed me, so I soon started my own library and have continued adding to it for the past ten years.

---

[1] Bishop Lance Webb, *Disciples for Life in the Age of Aquarius* (Waco, TX: Word Books, 1972), 12.

Aerobic Exercise: Sound Body, Sound Mind

About twenty-five years ago I began devoting the time before breakfast to a half hour of exercise, such as jogging, but now I devote the noon hour to aerobic exercise, usually swimming but occasionally jogging. I generally spend my lunch hour swimming since there is a pool nearby. Usually the exercise eliminates my hunger, but if not, a roll suffices. I tell my patients to keep walking shoes in their lockers at work and to use them to walk briskly for a half hour during their lunch break.

Aerobic exercise, such as cross-country running, builds endurance. Isometric exercise, such as power-lifting, on the other hand, builds muscle mass and strength. Aerobic exercise results in greater overall cardiovascular and biochemical advantages than isometric exercise. It must be emphasized that any form of exercise should be considered a prescription, unique for each individual, that must be defined following a review of the patient's medical history and the completion of the necessary physical and laboratory tests. I would suggest that aerobic exercise be one half hour daily. At the conclusion of the exercise one should feel "pleasantly out of breath" in order to obtain maximum benefits.

There are several advantages of aerobic exercise (I preach about these advantages about ten times a day to patients). In addition to relieving stress and burnout, there are other rewards:

1. Endorphins are enzymes secreted during aerobic exercise that act on the brain to give one energy and a sense of well-being that lasts a good part of the day.

2. Weight loss is best accomplished by being reasonable in the diet but more importantly by walking enough to be "pleasantly out of breath" at the conclusion of the walk (about two miles of brisk walking). One sixty-year-old patient, weighing 269 pounds, was initially upset when, instead of prescribing a "diet pill," I prescribed jogging shoes to be used for walking. She

lost a hundred pounds in one year. Her diet never changed, and she never missed one day of walking. She now weighs below 160 pounds and looks great.

3. Exercise time is an opportunity to reflect, pray, and be quiet. For this reason, it is important in most cases to walk alone. I always say, "It's your time, your speed, your place to walk." If your spouse wants to join you, and happens to be ready at the same time, go the opposite direction and wave. Walking together can decrease the benefits each of you receive. Walking speed varies between people, which can lead to one of you walking way ahead of the other in order to get the maximum benefit. It is easy to avoid this problem by walking in opposite directions around the block. (Besides, the neighbors won't think that you've had a fight if you do it this way, since you will have started together and ended together!)

4. Some of the biochemical advantages of exercise include a decrease of serum cholesterol and triglycerides and an increase in serum high density lipoprotein (HDL, the "good" cholesterol), which acts as a scavenger for cholesterol.

5. Your resting pulse and blood pressure will often decrease as a result of regular exercise, which ultimately leads to less work for the heart.

6. Blood platelets that clog up coronary arteries and cause thromboses (blockage of these arteries) become less sticky as a result of regular exercise, and they are, therefore, less likely to cause a problem.

7. People who exercise for any regular period of time tend to stop cigarette smoking. Sooner or later it will dawn on the smoker that it is counterproductive to smoke at the same time he or she is trying to build up endurance.

8. Excretion of adrenalin by-products into the urine, which is a result of exercise, appears to lead to less cardiac rhythm abnormalities, some of which can be dangerous.

Healing the Healer: Avoiding Burnout among Healers

A Circle of Prayer

An ideal prayer situation for avoiding burnout among healers such as physicians, clergy, nurses, social workers, and lay ministers, is one in which communication and support run in all directions. The clergy are patients for the physician; the physicians are parishioners for the clergy. Everyone has something to offer when it comes to healing and prayer. All members of the community can participate in this circle of prayer.

Traditionally, we expect the impossible from the clergy, praying for and ministering to the daily changing needs of all in their parish. Similarly, we expect health-care workers to give unceasingly. We expect sensitivity and compassion from our social workers without giving them adequate compensation. We must learn to give in all directions and remember the limitations of each of us alone.

There must be a two-way relationship in prayer between the three basic groups of people found among us: the clergy, health-care workers, and lay people (parishioners/patients). All three groups must recognize each other's needs and be sensitive to them. This means praying for and with each other, and in most cases, laying on of hands. Although praying for someone miles away is important, in one's own community it is preferable to be present physically, to be attentive to the person's individual needs, and to be able to actually touch him or her in a caring way.

As health-care providers, we don't have to be "certified" to be disciples. The clergy will still offer the sacraments, and physicians will still practice medicine. There is no competition involved. The common denominator is that we all are children of God. We all have been hurt or have had times of severe stress in the past or will in the future. No one is immune to this. We should be willing to share our hurts and our victories with fellow believers.

Henri Nouwen remarks that we must be willing to leave ourselves open to our fellow human beings and recognize that we, as healers, have the same wounds and require the same healing. He states, "... a shared pain is no longer paralyzing but mobilizing. ... Those very pains are transformed from expressions of despair into signs of hope."[2]

Spiritual Director

A spiritual director, who is either a layperson of strong spiritual background with whom you have kinship or a nun or priest, can be of benefit as well. The spiritual director acts also as a guidepost for our spiritual journey and occasionally may prevent us from being carried away in extremes of religious fervor. I am fortunate to have a spiritual director with whom I can share any need and from whom I can request prayer for these needs. Also, she lets me know about upcoming retreats, visiting clergy, and new books on spirituality, as well as other news that concerns spirituality. We discuss meditation and contemplation, and she often suggests good reference books. A spiritual director is interested in how you are experiencing prayer. Is prayer from the heart, or are too many distractions getting in the way? Has there been a dry spell where nothing seems to be happening and where your prayer life seems flat? How do you relate scripture to your life? These are the kinds of questions my spiritual director and I discuss. But perhaps most importantly, we pray regularly for each other's needs.

Centering Prayer

Centering prayer has had an important influence on me. A TM course I took many years ago introduced me to the technique of centering. Once I reach my spiritual core, a peaceful and

---

[2] Henri Nouwen, *The Wounded Healer* (Garden City, NY: Image Books, 1972), 93.

meditative state reached by means of words, scripture, music, or mental imaging, I select an intercessory prayer, repeat the Lord's Prayer, or just am quiet. Many monastic orders over the centuries have accomplished this centering with variations of the Jesus prayer. One variation is to say "Jesus" while inhaling quietly and "Abba" (Father) while exhaling quietly. Whatever method I use, centering prayer opens up to me an inner peace that "passeth all understanding." I frequently suggest to patients that they read Herbert Benson's book, *Relaxation Response*,[3] as a good way to learn the technique of centering.

Retreats

Retreats can be any size and may be oriented toward healing or to a wider base of prayer, silence, reflection, and meditation. A directed retreat may include spending one hour per day with an experienced spiritual director, usually a man or woman of the cloth. The rest of the day may be spent in reflection, meditation, contemplation, or study. The duration of a retreat can be a few hours, several weeks, or longer. I have found them to be very helpful, as I mentioned in chapter 3. The fruit of a retreat is the appreciation of what the Lord is doing in your life and the lives of fellow retreatants. By praying for one another, by praising God for what he has done in each person's life, and by sharing your life with others you can gain a spiritual dimension that otherwise is not attainable in the everyday world. You learn that you are not the only person who has hurts, anxieties, and problems; many of the retreatants do too. They have overcome them and can encourage you, or you, in turn, can encourage them with your victories. You learn to praise God in every circumstance, not just the good circumstances.

The retreat atmosphere is in many ways analogous to and serves the same purpose as the prayer group atmosphere. One advantage of a retreat is that there are retreat leaders using a definite format, who are experienced, able, and willing to guide the group in prayer, the laying on of hands, healing services, praise, songs, etc. A retreat allows you to get away from your

---

[3] Benson, Herbert. *Relaxation Response*. New York: William Morrow and Co., 1975.

normal environment, and this new environment produces less distractions and more concentration on what the Holy Spirit is doing in your life. As the retreatants open up, a oneness develops, a community of loving Christians, which is truly the Body of Christ. At the conclusion of the retreat, friendships often continue.

Fellow Christians are frequently at different places along their respective spiritual journeys. We learn that the Lord leads us to him along different paths and that it is important to be sensitive to this and to learn from each other. D. Elton Trueblood makes this point, "This is a world of emerging novelty, and God may speak to men in ways of which we have not dreamed. This, at least, is the view of revelation inherent in all spiritual religion."[4]

Books, Tapes, and Music

Spiritual books, tapes, and music all have important parts to play in keeping our spiritual fires aglow and batteries charged. I've listened to fine homilies and music on the car radio while driving to the ER in the middle of the night. I remember a minister patient of mine saying to me when I mentioned how difficult it can be to get up at 3:00 a.m. to admit someone to the hospital, "Bill, you are saved to serve." This is probably true for each of us irrespective of our vocation. The genuine pleasure exemplified by the retired men and women working as hospital volunteers illustrates this. They are happy to work, even though they are retired, in order to reach out to others.

Pilgrimages

Visits to the Holy Lands, Assisi, and Taizé have been special events for me, each having its own very special gift. The Holy Lands made the Bible come alive for me. My visit to Jerusalem, the Holy City and religious landmark for probably half of the world's population and home to all Christians, Jews,

---

[4] D. Elton Trueblood, *The Essence of Spiritual Religion* (New York: Harper & Brothers, 1936), 109.

and Moslems, was a remarkable experience. I felt like I was living the scriptures, especially when I visited the wailing wall, the Mount of Olives, and various churches, mosques, and temples. My visit to Assisi allowed me to experience the splendid peaceful atmosphere that reflects the peace of St. Francis. Because of its traditions and services that reflect the early church, Assisi is a bridge connecting the centuries. Here was something permanent that had survived the test of time. Taizé, a monastery in southeastern France, showed me the joy of brother- and sisterhood of Christians from all over the world. The pilgrims there were mainly men and women in their early twenties: an international ecumenical community of young Christians where national borders and origins play a secondary role. On any given weekend five thousand of them are there sharing, singing, and worshipping in many different languages. Between services prayer groups and small Bible study groups are held. I came away from Taizé with greater optimism for our world.

Religious Organizations

Being a member of the Third Order of St. Francis has brought many blessings to me. Membership in religious organizations can have a positive impact on renewal by providing an environment in which members can affirm one another and thus avoid burnout.

One Saturday not too long ago, about a dozen of us were having a retreat in a church outside of Philadelphia. We met in a small room that was used as a library and was part of the church complex. A First Order Franciscan priest had driven down from Long Island to be the retreat leader. We had been spending some time discussing Matthew 25, verses 31–46, relating these words to today's needs in our society. This discussion encompassed the poor, homeless, destitute, and hungry. Matthew 25.35: "For I was hungry and you gave me something to eat, I was thirsty and you gave me something to drink, I was a stranger and you invited me in."

During the discussion of this verse, suddenly we heard someone knocking on an outside door. After opening the door, my heart almost stopped when I saw a weary, middle-aged man, apparently a street person, standing in the cold. He asked if he could have something to eat. We invited him to come inside and join our Bible study group as it was almost time to take our lunch break. He was given an extra Bible and followed the readings along with us. At lunch time, he eagerly sat down with us in the parish kitchen. Those of us who brought our own sandwiches all offered a portion to him. I couldn't help smiling when I overheard him say, having been offered a peanut butter and jelly sandwich, "I've always hated peanut butter and jelly sandwiches ever since I was a kid." However, he had no difficulty in downing the rest of our offerings. After he had his fill of food and drink, he thanked us, quietly rose, opened the side door, and soon disappeared from view.

Following the lunch break, Matthew 25, verses 37–40 were especially poignant.

> Then the righteous will answer him, "Lord, when did we see you hungry and feed you, or thirsty and give you something to drink? When did we see you a stranger and invite you in, or needing clothes and clothe you? When did we see you sick or in prison and go to visit you?" The King will reply, "I tell you the truth, whatever you did for one of the least of these brothers of mine, you did for me."

I wonder how many times in the past I've passed by a needy person like this man. Could any one of them have been Christ? For all of us at the retreat, the text became more alive.

Saintly Encounters

God continues his work by constantly introducing to me many new friends I'll call "saints" because of their strong spiritual natures. One such person is Peter, who was a member of a Bible study group and who advised me to join the Third Order of St. Francis. Another such "saint" is Mary, who, upon hearing a talk I gave at a retirement village on spiritual healing, urged me to write a book about it. Another of my special friends is an evangelist minister who travels all over the globe but always stops by when he returns home so we can pray for each other's needs. All of us have special friends who serve as "saints" as we travel life's road. It seems that these people are sent to help us along the way much as we are sent to help others. I'll forever be grateful to those who have helped me on my way. As Barclay so aptly put it:

> The Christian life is a continuous going into the presence of God from the presence of men, and coming into the presence of men from the presence of God. . . . The rhythm of the Christian life is the alternative meeting with God in the secret place and serving men in the market place.[4]

This passage applies to retreats, as well as the less formal daily quiet meditation at home. Cervantes wrote, "Many are the roads by which God carries His own to heaven."

As I have tried to illustrate, there is a whole package of things that have nourished me spiritually, emotionally, and physically and have helped me to avoid burnout. All the techniques and resources mentioned above have helped me, and I plan to continue using or practicing them. For me this routine works and seems to keep me, at least so far, free from serious burnout. But I don't live in a vacuum; I live in the world. I must be very conscious of the need to balance my work with my family relationships, keep up with friends to the best of my ability, stay abreast of medical advances, and take part in recreational activities. What a delicate balancing act we all must go through. In this endeavor listening to the small inner voice of God is vital.

Professional Psychological Help

Psychiatrists and clinical psychologists are trained to help us sort out areas of confusion, depression, or anxiety in our

---

[5] William Barclay, *The Gospel of Mark*, The Daily Study Bible Series, revised edition (Philadelphia: Westminster Press, 1975), 155.

lives. In certain emotional situations, psychotherapy is critical and the use of psychiatric medications is very helpful. There are therapists who find prayer a most worthwhile adjunct to standard psychotherapy, especially after the patient has had time to become more rational in behavior and thought. Many psychologists and psychiatrists believe that the healing of emotionally upsetting events in the past is important but also believe that knowing that God loves and forgives us can bring about a deep spiritual healing that should not be underestimated.

Mind, Body, and Spirit

As said earlier, as healers we must address the whole patient: mind, body, and spirit. Each of us is composed of spirit (God within us), body, and mind. In order to be healthy, all three parts of us need to be maintained. We need quiet time daily to listen to God's voice within us. We must respect and care for our bodies by exercising and getting rest when we need it. We must also attend to our fears, anxieties, stresses, and emotions of all kinds. In some cases exercise, despite its role in promoting a sense of well-being, may not be enough to cope with life's upsets. Likewise, prayer may need to be supplemented by professional psychological help at times of crisis. An awareness of the whole person is very important for avoiding burnout. The effort required to keep the mind-body-spirit intact is considerable, but the result is well worth it.

How stress interrelates with physical health will be addressed in chapter 9, "Stress and the Immune System." Does stress lower the body's resistance to disease? Do inner peace and positive attitudes improve the body's ability to cope with health-threatening situations? These and related questions will be addressed at a more technical level by describing how the body's immune system reacts to favorable and unfavorable (stressful) states of mind.

7

Happiness Returns

Family Life

After a couple of years in my own spiritual desert (a place where all external trappings are stripped away, a place where we come face-to-face with our Lord, and, perhaps for the first time, are alone with him, a place where we sense his love, his grace, and his eternal presence), I gradually began the dating game again—a strange experience after twenty years of marriage. I began to regain my self-confidence with women and learned that I wasn't a "reject" after all. I will always appreciate those wonderful women who helped to bring light to a formerly dark place within me. Caring for someone and being cared for brought a whole new dimension to my life. At some point during this time, some mutual friends introduced me to Aline. The connection between us, in their minds, was that we had both just returned from retreats. Our friends thought we would have something in common right from the start. About one and a half years later, four years after the onset of my crisis, Aline and I were married.

At this writing, two of my children have finished college and are happily married. The third is finishing college now. The children have constantly been in my prayers and I am sure always will be. The children all turned out to be great kids, warm and loving individuals, and very fond of my wife, who feels the same about each of them.

After being married and living in my apartment for about one and a half years, Aline and I began to search for an affordable house, no easy task these days. We searched for one year, prayed for the right house and managed to miss four homes for various reasons including too low a bid, being twenty minutes late for a showing, and being one and a half days late in making an offer. We couldn't understand why the Lord let us down so many times, until, you guessed it, we found the one that turned out to be the best for our needs. It is a pleasant thirty-year-old ranch house that sits on a tiny hill and that initially needed a fair amount of work (like a new roof) and still needs more work (but our budget dictates which repairs we can make). The house is located on the outskirts of town on a quiet street and has a relatively large backyard that backs up against some woods. Deer, raccoon, birds, owls, rabbits, and squirrels can be found in the woods and in the backyard. There is a small garden of pachysandra in the back around some trees. My statue of St. Francis seems much at home there.

The children, their spouses, and visitors can now sleep on a bed or couch—no more sleeping on floors as was necessary in the apartment (unless there are an unusual number of guests all at once, in which case we make do with sleeping bags on the floor).

My wife commutes to New York and works as a broker selling residential real estate, which she had done in the past. She is good at her job and enjoys the people. Since she lived in New York for about ten years she has many old friends whom she can visit for lunch or over a cup of coffee from time to time. Though Aline enjoys her real estate career, her special interest is working for the poor.

Aline volunteers at Martin House, a church-run social service project, that arranges for tutoring, by volunteers, of disadvantaged children and also gives their mothers an opportunity to study for a high school equivalency diploma. Martin House, which has been in operation for the past several years, offers other services including repairing abandoned buildings and selling the rehabilitated homes at a reasonable rate to low-income families and helping people fix up each other's homes (since most banks will not give home improvement loans to poor people living in run-down housing). Not only houses, but many lives have been transformed by these programs. Martin House is a beacon in an otherwise dreary place. The Lord has heightened our sensitivities to the plight of the poor and homeless.

Our prayer life is a source of great strength for our union. We pray together often and find great peace in this sharing. Many friends, including religious, find in our home a place of peace and love—something I've prayed for and for which I'm very grateful.

I'm thankful that my ex-wife and I were at least successful as parents though unsuccessful as mates. I have always made it a point never to denigrate the children's mother, and I feel she has acted similarly. All too often in divorce the ex-spouses remain bitter and hostile, which is very hard on the children. I feel I have been blessed to have avoided this unpleasantness. It is important that children feel each parent is worthy of respect, and that children feel they are loved by each of their parents.

Professional Life

There are now three of us practicing as partners, and the patient load continues to grow. The partnership has resulted in more time off for each of us and is a pleasant change from the previous years. It has been nice to have colleagues in the same office with whom to exchange ideas regarding medical problems or just share everyday happenings.

The Lord Abiding in Us and We in Him

The point of this chapter is to give the reader hope that no matter how dark the night, joy comes in the morning. Don't give up. We must pray daily, as I try to do. Darkness can be a time of cleansing. Time alone in the desert seems to be necessary for further spiritual growth, at least it was for me.

Brother Lawrence, in his book, *Practicing the Presence of God*, discussed how pain and suffering can be great stimuli to spiritual growth. Suffering often brings humility and a change in perspective that help you to grow in God's grace. His life illustrates how suffering can lead to great peace.

Brother Lawrence was born in 1614, and as a young man became a brother in a monastery in Paris. For the first ten years there he suffered physically from arthritis and carried heavy burdens emotionally and spiritually. All the menial tasks at the monastery were assigned to him. One day he experienced a magnificent sense of inner peace—the presence of God. God was in him and he sensed he was in God. For the next forty years he lived in unity with God. He died in 1692. Brother Lawrence's letters have as much to teach us today as they did then. No matter what activity he was engaged in, it was done with a sense of being in God's presence and enduring love. He thought life's bad times were opportunities for spiritual growth and could lead to even greater ways of expressing God's glory. He wrote several letters to a friend who was a nun. One of these letters, written in 1690, says, "I have already told you in my last letter that He sometimes permits the body to suffer to cure the illness of our souls; be courageous, make a virtue of necessity." He goes on to say, "Love eases pain and when one loves God, one suffers for Him with joy and with courage." And later, "He is the Father of the afflicted, always ready to aid us, and He loves us infinitely more than we imagine.[1]

Albert E. Day, a Protestant theologian who was active in founding the DOC, beautifully describes this participation with God:

> Abiding in Him, prayer becomes communion, and service a sacrament. His abiding in us becomes the Presence for which our spirits cry, the comradeship which sweetens all loneliness, the victory which banishes all fear, the medicine which heals our diseases, the answer which resolves all tragedy.[2]

---

[1] Brother Lawrence, *Practicing the Presence of God*, John H. Delaney, trans. (Garden City, NY: Image Books, 1977), 92.

[2] Albert E. Day, *Discipline and Discovery* (Nashville, TN: The Parthenon Press, 1961), 127.

As healing progresses, we are able to reach out to others who may need our help. We are able to uplift others by our works and by our lives much as we have been uplifted. We are able to empathize better than before; we make our own journey, but we may, through prayer, become spiritual partners or friends with others along the way. A whole new dimension of healing opens up through prayer. These same individuals whom we touch and who touch us, in turn reach out to others. The power of prayer allows each one to begin to realize that God really does have a plan for each of us that will glorify him and bring purpose and fulfillment to our lives.

> But thanks be to God! He gives us the victory through our Lord Jesus Christ.

> 1 Corinthians 15.57

8

The Journey Continues

Praying Daily with Patients

Where have I been for the past several years and where am I going? I've become more open: less uptight with patients and therefore more vulnerable. Using discernment, I now pray two or three times a day with patients and will continue to do so in the future. I've seen the Lord work miracles not only in my own life but in the lives of others, and these miracles go on day after day. I've tried to be more attentive, talk less, and listen more to my patients.

Dietrich Bonhoefer recognized the need for us to listen. In *Life Together* he wrote:

> Many people are looking for an ear that will listen. They do not find it among Christians, because these Christians are talking when they should be listening. But he who can no longer listen to his brother will soon be no longer listening to God either; he will be doing nothing but prattle in the presence of God too.[1]

---

[1] Dietrich Bonhoefer, *Life Together* (New York: Harper Brothers, 1954), 97–98.

A pundit once wrote, "God gave us two ears to listen with, only one mouth to speak with." At times one would guess it was the other way around.

Prayers can be silent; another person's mere presence, a hug, or an empathetic touch can serve as a silent prayer. I often pray silently if I feel that the patient is not open to audible prayer. Prayers may also be audible, however, spoken through the Holy Spirit. These prayers are always on target. Laying on of hands has become virtually routine with my prayers. Patients pray for me as well. I say many prayers in my office with the door closed or at the hospital bedside when alone with my patients and occasionally with family members and close friends also. In order to avoid extraneous distractions, I feel the noise and curiosity of passersby should be excluded. Privacy in prayer, therefore, is important. These prayers may be prayers of intercession, prayers of affirmation, or prayers of thanksgiving and praise. Often all of these prayers are used depending on how the Spirit moves us. I have never said a steamroller prayer, which overwhelms the sensitivities of the patient, because the Spirit is always there with guidance and discernment.

We share the results of prayers at our next meeting. Knowing the Lord has his plan for each of us, we acknowledge it. If the prayers bring unexpected results, we continue to pray for his plan and remain open to it. When prayers are answered as we had hoped, we rejoice and share this joy with others. We need, as Christians, to witness to others what God has done. Several people besides myself, such as relatives of the patient, a prayer group, friends, clergy, and other paramedical or health-care professionals, have also prayed with my patients and me. In these instances, there is a greater spiritual energy from the laying on of hands because the Lord is working through several people in order to flood the patient with his healing power.

As you can see, there has been quite a transformation in my daily practice of medicine. I've come a long way from being closed up, uptight, and afraid to reach out. I am now tuned in and more attentive to my patients. I no longer say the successful outcome of a complex case is just a lucky break. I appreciate more how wonderfully made our bodies are and how every healing is beautiful. I appreciate God's presence in all healing, even healing of minor illnesses and injuries.

Exercise and the Temple of the Body

There is much energy expended in a busy practice. As I get older and some of my friends and patients die, I appreciate my life more and more and become very conscious of my own mortality and of the vocation given to me by God: being a channel for healing. I've been privileged, as have most physicians who have been in practice, to touch the lives of patients. As long as I have something to contribute while here on earth, I feel our Lord will continue to use me for his glory. What continues to amaze me is the energy the Lord has given me to continue to work a full day after only a few hours' sleep the night before. He has also given me excellent health, and I've disciplined myself to preserve "the temple of the body" over these many years. It must be difficult to tell people to stop smoking and to exercise if you, the physician, fail to heed your own advice.

Aerobic exercise will continue to be important for me. I manage to compete in four or five swim meets in my age group in the U. S. Masters Swimming Association each year. There are so many benefits from aerobic exercise that I will continue to practice what I preach about exercise as long as possible. It is prudent to take care of the body we have inherited. A healthy body houses a healthy mind and spirit in most cases, and we can be more effective disciples for others when we are healthy.

To replenish the energy, to charge the batteries, I spend a half hour in the morning after a light breakfast reading scripture and in prayer. This is vital for me. An inner strength and peace remain with me all day despite the challenges and hectic schedule of a typical work day.

This reading practice has evolved from my earlier days of reading a daily missal for a few minutes at breakfast. With the children now grown, there is an opportunity for quiet, meditation, and listening to God. During my reflection a host of answers to problems, questions, and decisions become clearer as the Lord speaks to these issues and guides me. Scripture says, "Here I am! I stand at the door and knock. If anyone hears my voice and opens the door, I will come in and eat with him, and he with me" (Revelation 3.20). You can't hear the knock if you aren't quiet.

Frequent meditation leads logically to leading a contemplative life, which is an active awareness of God's presence in everything and everyone. I find myself now reading more and more about being a contemplative person in the "real" world. In order to be contemplative I must have an unusual reconciliation and unity with God, a constant communication with God, a feeling that he is part of me and I a part of him and the rest of his creation. This communication and contemplation create a unity—a bonding of myself, God, and his world. The result is love in action.

Daily renewal at home and renewal in more formal, organized ways are both important. Among the latter, as mentioned earlier, joining the Third Order of St. Francis has been important to me because I have tried to follow his rule of life—a life built on simplicity, joy, praising God, humility, justice, and being of service. In this organization, a spiritual director and a counselor help, advise, encourage, and pray with you during the postulate, novitiate, and, finally, professed stages.

My wife, Aline, has blessed me with her many friends in the religious community including nuns, priests, and bishops. She also shares my time in the morning for prayer and devotion. She has joined a small group of Manhattanville alumnae who meet at regular intervals for an evening of prayer, sharing, and reflection. It is largely through her efforts that we have become friends of two inner-city black girls, ages eight and eleven, whom we met through Martin House. Aline frequently takes them on a Saturday afternoon outing to a museum or concert or brings them back to our home to play and stay for a cookout, if the weather permits. One of the girls lives in a small two-story house that is home to eighteen people, three generations from one family. Like many poverty-ridden cities, the problem of drugs surrounds these children from all sides. The girls' families appreciate these small trips and welcome the opportunity for them to see new places. Our prayer is that in some way we can help the girls aim for higher education and a better life.

Sowing Seeds in Practice

We all have opportunities in our various occupations to sow spiritual seeds. An eye surgeon I know prays with his patients before each cataract operation; a businessman prays with his office staff at the beginning of each work day; I understand that there is a Congressional prayer breakfast group that has been in operation in Washington, D. C. for years, and so on.

I continue to have opportunities during my practice to drop seeds. Opportunities arise from time to time during hospital teaching rounds, during lectures, or during emergencies in the CCU, or in the office. These seeds are dropped gently and without fanfare; some germinate and some undoubtedly do not. Some are planned, and some are spontaneous.

For example, one lecture I give to medical students consists of listing the factors that influence the development of coronary artery disease and heart attacks. In addition to the well-known roles played by diet, tobacco, lack of exercise, high blood pressure, obesity, alcohol abuse, and drug abuse, I often touch on stress and its multiple adverse effects. This topic inevitably leads me to mention how necessary it is for all of us to have a quiet time in our hectic life—a time to be still for twenty-five or thirty minutes a day. I go on to end the lecture by saying that during this time one might meditate or even pray quietly. Most of the students in the class leave when I'm finished. Perhaps two will have a thoughtful look for a moment, and perhaps one will come up and ask me to say a word more about how prayer fits in with the practice of medicine. I then mention the need for treating the whole person—mind, body, and spirit. Often I mention a case that is in the hospital at the time where prayer is being used in addition to the usual medical treatment.

Occasionally, as will be mentioned later, a patient in the ICU or CCU takes an unexpected turn for the worse. If, after ordering all necessary medical treatment, the situation is still grave, using discernment I pray quietly with the patient. Some time later, if the particular condition has improved, despite what appeared to be an almost hopeless situation, the intern might ask what I think made the difference. I'm not embarrassed to look him or her in the eyes and say, "We prayed." In cases like this, I often ask myself, "Did I go far enough?" "Should I have talked more about the power of prayer?" I don't want to be thought of as an overly pious physician, so usually I use discernment to determine how far I should go in the particular case. More than once I've heard, after mentioning that prayer was part of the treatment, "I never heard an attending physician say that before!" Once, much to my surprise, the house officer replied that prayer helped him or her or a family member in a similar critical condition. One time, a house officer said he and a few of the nurses had been praying with a patient of mine, and he hoped I didn't mind! I, of course, assured him that I strongly believe in prayer. The Holy Spirit is working through many people and in many ways. Trueblood has this to say about the sowers of the spiritual seed:

> If a missionary is one who nourishes the Seed in others, we need missionaries everywhere, and there is no more noble profession. This might take on many forms, such as medicine or politics or business.[2]

Although I have amply stressed being quiet in order to hear what God may be saying, I would like also to mention the importance of being tuned in to the Lord's presence. Quiet time is a time you schedule for prayer and meditation and is in a place without distractions. Being tuned in is remaining open to God's voice even when you are busy, often working with many distractions. It is being open to your intuition, listening always despite the distraction of the "real" world, not letting your daily physical concerns overshadow the true concerns of your spirit.

Being Tuned in to God

A few years ago, I had the good fortune to be with Bishop Robert Morneau, a longtime friend of my wife, Aline. He led me on a directed retreat for about one week in the summer at St. Norbert's Seminary in the Green Bay area of Wisconsin. It was a deep spiritual journey and something that the Lord had led me to do. While having lunch with a handful of laity there, a gentleman sat down next to me. He had just undergone open heart bypass surgery in Milwaukee. He said, "Even though I live only a few miles away from St. Norbert's, the Lord led me to this place before returning home." He had a bundle of questions about his

---

[2] Trueblood, *Essence of Spiritual Religion*, 151.

heart surgery and fears about his future health. He said that he wished the doctors had been able to spend more time explaining to him what happens to patients after surgery, what activities he should do, and what life-style changes he needed to make. He then asked me what kind of work I did. When I said I was a cardiologist, he gasped and said that he knew there was a reason for his being drawn to this place directly from the hospital. I answered most of his questions to the best of my ability. He apparently had an excellent local physician who would continue his care. He stayed at the seminary for only a couple of days, but, toward the end of his stay, he seemed reassured. We both remarked that the Lord often places people in our lives as agents for his grace. We prayed for each other and parted. I believe we were equally enriched by this encounter.

How many times have you and I ignored the inner voice urging us to make that phone call to a particular person or to write that letter or make that visit? How many times has that one crucial opportunity been lost forever, passed by, been acted upon too late, never to return again? On the other hand, do you recall the joy, the satisfaction, and the relief when you did listen and did react to God's urging?

Three instances recently occurred in my life that all centered around God's attempt to speak to me. These are examples of being tuned in, two instances when I did respond and one when I did not. You undoubtedly can recall similar experiences in your life as well.

Not too long ago, having just finished a rather exhausting Saturday morning of office hours, I was eagerly looking forward to relaxing at home. As I started for my car in the nearby parking lot, something inside of me told me to go to the ICU before doing anything else and to go there right then. Ted was my only patient in the unit. He was a sixty-five-year-old ex-smoker with severe emphysema, recovering without major complications from pneumonia. I had already checked on him earlier in the morning, and he had been in satisfactory condition. No one had called from the unit saying his condition had deteriorated in any way, so why was I being urged to go there? Nevertheless, after reflecting on this for a few minutes, I decided I would take one more look at him, and, since the cafeteria was nearby, I could get a bite to eat right afterward.

No sooner had I reached his bedside than Ted suddenly gasped, turned cyanotic, and virtually stopped breathing. His jaws were tightly locked, closing his airway. He slipped into an unconscious state right before my eyes. Luckily a surgeon was nearby, who performed an emergency tracheotomy that saved Ted's life. He was very weak and undoubtedly had choked on a food particle. He was discharged a couple of weeks later. Could this all be coincidental or was the Lord telling me something? Needless to say, I was thankful I did make that ICU stop. I never did stop by the cafeteria. Somehow I forgot all about the snack.

Another example of being nudged by that small inner voice occurred only a couple of weeks ago. My habit has always been to see my hospital patients the first thing in the morning before starting my office hours. On this particular morning, I was a bit late for the office, having experienced a number of unexpected problems among some other hospital patients. A lovely seventy-two-year-old woman, Elaine, who had been a patient of mine for about fifteen years, had recently been diagnosed as having acute leukemia and was hospitalized for intensive chemotherapy under the care of one of our oncologists.

Over the years, I've always tried to make an effort to see my patients who are admitted for a different specialty, such as surgery, or in this case, oncology. These visits are "social calls" to check on the patients' conditions and how they are coping. The inner voice said, "Visit Elaine even though you are pressed for time and rushing to get to the office." Part of me responded, "It would be more convenient to see her at noon or at the end of the day." Still, the voice came back with, "Go now." As I entered the room, Elaine disarmed me with her warm, friendly manner and remarked how happy she was to see me. She was a very spiritual woman and over the years frequently had quite openly discussed how much God had done for her. We stayed together, holding hands and having a good conversation; it was truly a prayerful visit and lasted about twenty minutes. She was alert throughout this time, and, although she was not feeling well, she did not appear to be critically ill. At the conclusion of our visit, she mentioned how much the visit had meant to her and once again thanked me for stopping in to see her. When she asked if I would visit her again, I reassured her that I would stop by every day during her hospital stay. As I left the room she waved, and, reflecting a certain inner peace, she smiled again and laid her head back on the pillow. Fifteen minutes later, the hospital floor nurse called my office to say that Elaine had quietly died quite unexpectedly. I thanked God that I had not waited to visit her later in the day.

Despite the proven validity of my inner voice, I once failed to listen to it. To make matters worse, this occurred only a few days after my visit with Elaine. A dear friend and colleague of twenty years was slowly dying of metastatic cancer in a nearby city. It was difficult to communicate with him by phone, and my letters were not answered. I knew after visiting with him soon after the diagnosis was made that he preferred to handle his crisis in his own private way. Nevertheless, we did subsequently enjoy a visit over lunch in a local restaurant, which helped to keep our relationship strong during that troubled time.

It had been one of those extra busy weeks in the hospital and the office. I kept hearing the small inner voice telling me to write Jim a note of encouragement letting him know again how much I cared—some sort of note to show I was thinking about him. The week was slipping by, and I still had not written him. On Thursday nights I have evening hours, so by the time I returned home that Thursday, it was 9:30 p.m, and I only had time to relax a bit and go to bed. The first thing I did on Friday morning was to write the long-delayed note and mail it. In the middle of the afternoon, I received a phone call from a mutual friend that Jim had died that same Friday morning. Although he never lived to read the letter, my consolation is that at least he knew how I felt over the years. But how much better it would have been to have written this reaffirming letter earlier in the week!

We don't always listen to the Lord when he tries to speak to us, or we may hear him but fail to act. As James said, "Do not merely listen to the word, and so deceive yourselves. Do what it says" (James 1.22). When we do listen and do react to God's word, the results can be very, very gratifying. I've come to the realization that we must continually strive to live in God's presence and always listen to his small inner voice no matter how busy and complicated our lives may be. This means that we must learn to be tuned in constantly, as we attempt to live in his presence.

Bioengineering Advances and the Physician's Image

Although the scientific advances in medicine have virtually revolutionized patient treatment, it seems that personal care for patients has actually decreased. There is an ever-widening gap between the hurting patient and the caring physician. Unless this issue can be addressed in the near future, the doctor-patient bond will suffer, and the joy of practicing medicine will diminish. I recently overheard a conversation between two medical students in the hospital. "Why bother listening for the details of the heart murmur when an echocardiogram with doppler will give the answer?" one of the students asked his classmate. In other words, why touch the patient with a stethoscope when a bioengineering tool can be used? Why take a medical history from a patient personally, when a computer can take the history? The gap between patient and physician is growing wider.

It is obvious to those of us who have been in the medical field for any length of time that personally taking the patient's history is vital. You find out which areas are emotionally charged for the patient, how the patient copes with stress, and in general what makes the patient tick. The patient likewise evaluates the physician. Is he or she attentive? sensitive? thorough? With the item-check questionnaire in which the physician, in order to save time, asks only about items #23 and #58 because they were not checked off as "normal," there is no opportunity to have a conversation or get to know each other at all. Both parties suffer: the physician does not get a complete picture of the patient, which may reduce his or her ability to care for the patient's health, and the patient does not get to know the physician, which may result in dissatisfaction and mistrust.

Patients today read a lot about the new advances in bioengineering and are especially interested in those tools that apply to them personally. I help foster this interest by, among other things, showing my patients their electrocardiogram strips and explaining what the readings mean. By explaining to patients on what criteria I base my medical decisions, I involve them more in their own health care. Instead of alienating patients, the new diagnostic tools can help patients feel more in control of their health care and more in touch with their physician. I recommend that physicians take the time in this way to try to close the gap between their patients and them.

The Dean of Duke Medical School, Doyle G. Graham, addressed this issue in an interview with my son William B. Haynes for the Duke *Dialogue* in September of 1987. He said,

> Technology is advancing at a dizzying pace, and it is easy for the public and physicians to be dazzled by the flashing lights, and lose interest in the image of the caring physician.[3]

Off-Hours Healing Ministry

I hope to continue to say yes when friends or acquaintances going through circumstances similar to mine ask if I will help. A one-on-one healing ministry or support system carried on during after hours and over supper has developed into a significant offshoot of my practice. During this time I listen attentively to the friend or acquaintance discuss his or her problem, and I often suggest tapes, books, retreats, or exercise that are appropriate for that person's needs. In many cases, I use laying on of hands and prayer. The joy of this activity is seeing God slowly transform an individual to the point where he or she goes out to help others; they in turn help others, the books and tapes are passed on, and so on. Usually there are two or three individuals currently on my prayer and supper list at any one time. With the aid of appropriate support, sharing, and praying, healing begins. And ever so gradually each, in turn, is able to reach out to help others. They have become true disciples, giving credit to the Holy Spirit, the Comforter, at all times.

---

[3] William B. Haynes, "Graham Stresses Ethics and Values in Medical School," Duke *Dialogue*, 11 September, 1987.

9

Stress and the
Immune System

There is an intense interest today in studying the influence of stress on the immune system. Does stress unfavorably affect the body's resistance to disease? If so, how does this occur? Similarly, physicians and researchers are trying to discover the influence of inner peace and positive attitudes on the immune system. Can they promote wellness and increase the body's resistance to disease? A number of physiological tests on animals and humans have demonstrated that state of mind has a great impact on physical health. Though the mechanisms that allow spiritual and mental health to affect physical health have not been discovered, the connection between mind and body is clearly a strong one and must be addressed by healers.

Promoting wellness has many rewards besides the obvious benefit to the individuals concerned. Better general health would reduce absenteeism and control medical costs, thus lowering insurance rates and medical fees. Physicians must help patients to change poor life-styles, which are often the cause of ill health. Improvements in quality of life are closely connected to improvements in health and vice versa.

In order to more fully discuss the relationship of stress and physical health, the following sections will be somewhat technical. I have tried to use the clearest and most accessible terms.

How does the immune system work? In simple terms, when a bacterial infection starts within the body, circulating white blood cells, called granulocytes, are drawn to the site of the infection. The granulocyte has the job of ingesting the bacteria that are causing the infection. The products of the dead bacteria are then passed into the circulation system where another white blood cell, called a lymphocyte, acts upon the dead bacteria. Lymphocytes come in two forms: the T lymphocyte, which becomes sensitive to the invading organism and prevents future infection by directly attacking the cell membrane of each invading bacterial cell; and the B lymphocyte, which produces circulating immune proteins called gamma globulins, which also act as fighters against future infection. Gamma globulins are the antibodies found in our blood stream after we have recovered from an infection such as the measles.

In recent years, researchers have been turning their attention toward the effect that a sense of inner peace and the ability to cope well with stress might have on the immune system. Many medical centers across the nation are finding that aerobic exercise and relaxation techniques do have beneficial effects. These positive effects are apparent not only in the sense of well-being the patients have, but also in an increase in T lymphocyte production. By studying subjects over a five-year period, Sheldon Cohen, a psychologist working in England, found that there was a relationship between stress and a high frequency of colds.[1] There were fewer colds among subjects having strong social support systems or caring family members. Neil Schneiderman and colleagues at the University of Miami Medical School found that by employing relaxation techniques, stress management, and aerobic exercise, there was a 10–14% increase in T lymphocyte production among subjects with positive blood tests for the HIV virus who had not yet contracted AIDS.[2] This has important implications for AIDS patients since their immune systems are deficient. At this time researchers and physicians hope to delay the onset of AIDS in patients infected

---

[1] Daniel Goleman, "Researchers Find that Optimism Helps the Body's Defense System," *New York Times*, 20 April 1989, Health section.
[2] Ibid.

with HIV until better treatment is available. Increasing the production of T lymphocytes may help.

Until recently, there has been a big gap between psychologists, who deal with emotions in their patients, and immunologists, who deal with the body's resistance to disease. Over the past few years, there has been a merger of sorts between these two disciplines, and the new specialty, "psycho-immunology," has been born. Dr. Mary Ann Fletcher, director of the clinical immunology laboratory at the University of Miami, said in a New York Times interview, "Immunologists have tended to be rather suspicious of the whole idea, but as people have begun to put it to the test, it's become an area that's taken seriously by more and more people in the field."[3]

The subject of stress and its effects on the body is complex and under continuous investigation. Physiological responses have been demonstrated in animals and humans as long as fifty years ago. Studies were made on people under emotional, rather than physical, stress, including medical students before final exams, coaches and oarsmen before the annual Yale-Harvard crew race, and relatives of ER patients. Subjects under stress experienced increased amounts of adrenal gland hormones in blood and urine.[4]

Most workers who study stress would agree that stress is a force that affects the body. The effect may even be positive in that it may help in reaching some goal. Whether the stress in a given situation acts to help us or to harm us frequently revolves around our ability to cope or not. In this discussion I am using the word "stress" to mean noxious stimulus, one that has deleterious or adverse effects on the nervous system. This kind of stress is the result of a poor coping mechanism.

How does the body handle an acute threat to its life? The autonomic nervous system responds to a threat by secreting adrenalin from the adrenal gland, which prepares the body for flight or fight. This response is not intended to be a long-standing one; the stressful situation should soon be resolved

---

[3] Ibid.
[4] George W. Thorne, Dalton Jenkins, John C. Laidlaw, Redrick C. Goetz and William Reddy, "Response of the Adrenal Cortex to Stress in Man," *Trans. Assoc. of American Physicians* 66 (1953): 48–64.

either by a fight or by running away. Unfortunately not all stressful situations today can be handled as they were thousands of years ago when most threats were direct physical dangers to our lives. What happens to the frustrated worker who cannot afford to leave his continuously stressful job? How can we deal with long-term anger? Fighting is not usually a viable solution. The body responds to perpetual stress by secreting another hormone from the adrenal gland, cortisone, which can eventually lead, when in high concentration in the blood stream, to increased blood pressure, peptic ulcers, and heart attacks. Immune responses can vary depending on the type of stress and the ability to cope with it. Mark L. Laudenslager and his team found that inability to cope with very stressful situations led to suppression of lymphocyte proliferation.[5] Steven E. Locke and his group reported decreased T cell activity during certain times of stress.[6] As would be expected, the opposite conditions, namely good attitudes, positive thinking, spiritual resources, and exercise, can relieve this depression of the immune system. The exact mechanism that controls this phenomenon is unknown at present but under vigorous study.

Other researchers have noticed that severe stress caused by loss of spouse, divorce, loss of job, or other traumatic changes may result in many different illnesses related to the breakdown of the immune response. To date, there is no irrefutable proof that stress causes cancer, but psychological and social situations may accelerate tumor growth according to Leo Stolbach and Ursula Brandt.[7]

S. Greer and his team noted that there are three factors associated with prolonged survival of women in the early stages (stage one or two) of breast cancer.[8]

---

[5] Mark L. Laudenslager, Susan M. Ryan, Robert C. Drugan, Richard L. Hyson, and Steven F. Maier, "Coping and Immunosuppression: Inescapable, but not Escapable, Shock Suppresses Lymphocyte Proliferation," *Science* 221 (1983): 568–70.

[6] Steven E. Locke, Linda Kraus, Jane Leserman, and R. Michael Williams, "Life Changes Stress, Psychiatric Symptoms, and Natural Killer Cell Activity," *Psychosomatic Med.* 46 (Sept./Oct. 1984): 441–53.

[7] Leo Stolbach and Ursula Brandt, *Stress and Breast Cancer*, C. L. Cooper, ed. (New York: John Wiley and Sons, Ltd., 1988.), 3–24.

[8] S. Greer, T. Morris, and K. W. Pettingale, "Psychological Response to Breast Cancer: Effect on Outcome," *Lancet* vol. 2 (1979): 785–87.

1. The will to live.
2. The ability to express emotions throughout most of the patient's adult life.
3. The presence of support groups and social contacts during the illness.

The patients who exhibited the opposite of these behaviors or conditions generally had a poorer prognosis. Similar findings relating stress to poor prognosis in cases of breast cancer were noted by James E. Talmadge and W. Gregory Alvord.[9]

There is increasing interest in the relationship between chronic emotional distress and cancer, though as yet there is no solid proof linking the two. R. B. Shekelle and his team performed psychological studies on two thousand workers at Western Electric and followed their health records over the following seventeen years. The Minnesota Multiphasic Personality Inventory (a psychological questionnaire that rates a subject's optimism) was employed as a baseline at the beginning of the study between 1957 and 1958. The odds of dying from cancer increased twofold among those who scored high in the category of depression.[10] More studies of this type are sorely needed.

O. Carl Simonton, Stephanie Matthews-Simonton, and T. Flint Sparks have done impressive work in the treatment of cancer patients. They employ a relaxation and imaging technique. In this technique, the patient relaxes and focuses on a mental image, such as white blood cells destroying the cancer cells, and imagines this as actually occurring. This treatment, in addition to the standard treatments, achieved greater success than the standard treatments alone.[11]

Although the precise link between stress and the biochemical immune responses of the body is not clear at this time, it is clear, nevertheless, that there is a connection, and that stress and

---

[9] James E. Talmadge and W. Gregory Alvord, "Stress Factors and Breast Cancer Outcome," *Journal Clinical Oncology* 5 (March 1987): 333–34.

[10] Richard B. Shekelle, William J. Raynor, Jr., Arian M. Ostfeld, David C. Garron, Linas A. Bieliauskas, Shuguey C. Liu, Carol Maliza, and Oglesby Paul, "Psychological Depression and Seventeen-year Risk of Death from Cancer," *Psychosomatic Med.* 43 (1981): 117–25.

[11] O. Carl Simonton, Stephanie Matthews-Simonton, and T. Flint Sparks, "Psychological Intervention in the Treatment of Cancer," *Psychosomatics* 21 (1980): 226–33.

inner peace stand at opposite poles. Stress is a negative force, decreasing body defenses, and inner peace is a positive force, increasing our resistance to illness. Evidence is accumulating that scientifically connects our thought processes to the activity of lymphocytes, gamma globulins, and adrenal gland hormones, in short, to our resistance to disease. Prayer groups, support groups, hobbies, vacations, behavior modification techniques, TM, relaxation response, exercise, and a generally nurturing and supportive environment can relieve stress and, therefore, should be encouraged by health-care providers.

For the first time, we are beginning to understand the relationship between emotional and spiritual health and physical health. We are discovering biochemical reactions to mental conditions. I hope that the cases in this book have demonstrated the power of prayer and the power of God's love and grace to heal those who are suffering. If the actual biochemical effects of healing prayer and peace can be discovered, so much the better. Perhaps then the skeptics among us will be convinced, and prayer will be used more frequently. I believe prayer works and I will continue to employ it in my own life as well as in patient care.

10

A Final Thought: The Lord Guides Us

It is virtually impossible to have any sense of wholeness or integration without God's active partnership in our lives. He must be the pilot guiding us along the journey to wholeness (the journey to holiness) as our hearts yearn to be more and more like him. I have come to know an inner peace since I began turning over control of my life to God.

I hope that my inner peace will allow me to be used as a channel for healing. A harassed physician can convey to his patients just that—harassment and turmoil rather than peace. Daily prayer and quiet time keep the inner fire burning, the batteries charged. It must be emphasized that this practice must be daily and ongoing because each day we are being confronted with new stresses, new challenges, and frequently new wounds that need healing.

When dealing with my own problems in life or when helping others carry their burdens, the following quotation from Isaiah gives me comfort:

Although the Lord gives you the bread of adversity and the water of affliction, your teachers will be hidden no more; with your own eyes you will see them. Whether you turn to the right or to the left, your ears

will hear a voice behind you, saying, "This is the way;
walk in it." . . . He will also send you rain for the seed
you sow in the ground, and the food that comes from
the land will be rich and plentiful.

Isaiah 30.20–21,23

The bread of suffering mixed with our tears is transformed
into the bread of life and nourishment. If we listen to our Lord,
he will lead us out of the dark night of sorrow into new life,
through his grace and ever-present love. Our tears are replaced
by rain, and the good works we do for his glory result in a life
that is blessed and rewarding.

How difficult it is to say in the middle of life's darkest place,
"Thank you Lord." It's hard to even conceive of thanking God
for suffering. One can only begin to think of thanking God for
a painful situation by stubbornly repeating over and over again
the truth that God has a perfect plan for each of us. Even so, you
still ask, "Where is the plan? Where is God?" I remember the
deep sorrow I felt one night while jogging. The tears were
flowing down my cheeks, but I still thanked God for being
present because I believed he was there. But I also felt I needed
a sign, a ray of light, something to give me encouragement. In
these times of darkness it is hard to keep a sense of humor, a
sense of perspective. I was reminded of that fact and reminded
of the importance of not taking oneself too seriously when I saw
a refrigerator magnet that said, "Lord give me patience, but
please hurry up."

After a time of despair and pain I returned to the light, and
I affirmed and witnessed many others coming back to the light.
The darkness did disappear; the light did come. There is inner
peace; there is growth; miracles can happen; healings do occur;
prayers are heard; and all for one thing—to help others and
thereby glorify God as we live in him and he in us.

Praise be to the God and the Father of our Lord Jesus
Christ, the Father of compassion and the God of all
comfort, who comforts us in all our troubles, so that we
can comfort those in any trouble with the comfort we
ourselves have received from God.

2 Corinthians 1.3–4

APPENDIXES A–D

A

Some Questions about
Prayer in Medicine

1. How can physicians who don't believe in God help patients who do?

If a doctor believes in some Higher Authority or Supreme Being he or she may be more attentive to the patient's own spirituality or religious tradition and see spirituality as an ally in the healing process. A doctor who does not have these beliefs may, nonetheless, be willing to call in or suggest seeing a clergy member of the patient's tradition in a case where the patient has forgotten this source of healing. An open-minded physician cannot discount the positive effects of prayer on patients who desire it.

2. How should prayer and stress reduction be addressed in medical school or at the postgraduate level?

There are courses now being given in both medical school and at the postgraduate level dealing with stress management. Robert Elliot, M.D., has given excellent courses every summer in Jackson Hole, Wyoming, sponsored by the American College of Cardiology. There is so much sensitivity about the separation of church and state in this country that the issue of prayer is quite charged. I feel that the best way to discuss or teach prayer is to reserve it for those times when the individual students are in a "safe place," i.e., among members of their own religious tradition. There are organization such as the Christian Medical Foundation that give ample opportunity for both students and doctors in practice to learn firsthand about prayer. For now, it seems that dropping seeds about prayer among students or house officers is an effective method of spreading the word. Another option for opening up this discussion could be to offer an elective seminar or class for those interested in prayer. Needless to say, intuition plays a major role in broaching this subject because it is all too easy to appear to be proselytizing.

3. *How can prayer as a part of medical practice be administered, controlled, or regulated by hospitals, or should it be?*

Prayer, both inside and outside of the hospital, is too personal for any regulation by the hospital or other authorities. I suppose a situation could occur, though I've never heard of one, in which some fanatical individual, totally insensitive to the patients' wishes, attempted to force prayer or his own beliefs upon every one of his patients. This behavior is quite contrary to the ideas and examples set forth in this book. The best way to handle this situation, should it ever occur, would be to ask the individual to leave.

I have found it best generally not to tell anyone in the hospital when I pray with patients. Prayer is best done in private, which usually means pulling the curtain around the hospital bed. Besides the importance of privacy as a service to the patient's dignity, privacy is important because it is so hard to concentrate when there are many distractions (as there are on any busy medical floor).

In summary, it seems best to leave the matter of prayer in medicine to the patient's own clergy member or physician whom he or she trusts and to continue the policy (or lack thereof) as it now is, that is, a quiet and private affair between the healer (physician or clergy member), the patient, and the Lord.

B
Christian Healing
Organizations

1. Association of Christian Therapists (ACT)
     3700 East Avenue, Rochester, NY 14618
2. Christian Medical Foundation (CMF)
     7522 North Himes Avenue, Tampa, FL 33614
3. Disciplined Order of Christ
     James Wagner, Executive Director
     1908 Grand Avenue, P.O. Box 189
     Nashville, TN 37202-0189
4. Graymoor Christian Unity Center
     Atonement Friars, Garrison, NY 10524
5. Sacred Heart Institute of Healing
     Rev. Gerald Ruanc, Ph.D., Director
     315 First Street, Westfield, NJ 07090
6. School of Pastoral Care
     c/o Rev. Edward A. Rouffy, Registrar
     P.O. Box 96, Castle Rock, CO 80104
7. Society of St. Francis in the American Province
     Little Portion Ferry, P.O. Box 399
     Mt. Sinai, NY 11766
8. The Upper Room
     1908 Grand Avenue, P.O. Box 189
     Nashville, TN 37202-0189

C
Tapes for Meditation
and Spiritual Growth

1. Groeschel, Benedict. "Come to Me." Kansas City, MO: National Catholic Reporter Publishing Company, 1982.
2. "Resurrexit," Taizé, France 71520: Les Presses de Taizé, 1984, imported by G.I.A. Publications, Inc., Chicago.
3. Moreau, Robert. "Spirituality and Human Growth." Canfield, OH: Alba House Cassettes, 1982.
4. Scheihing, Theresa. "Centering Meditations with Music: The Beautiful Earth." Kansas City, MO: National Catholic Reporter Publishing Company, 1982.

D
Christian Journals
and Devotional Guides

1. The Daily Study Bible Series, revised edition, William Barclay, Philadelphia: The Westminster Press, 1975.
2. *Daily Word*, Unity Village, MO 64065.
3. *Fellowship in Prayer*, 291 Witherspoon Street, Princeton, NJ 08542-9946
4. *Living with Christ*, P.O. Box 9700, Terminal, Ottawa, Canada K1G 4B4
5. *St. Joseph Weekday Missal*, Vol. I and II. New York: Catholic Book Publishing Company, 1975.
6. *Sojourners*, Box 29272, Washington, DC 20017
7. *The Upper Room*, 1908 Grand Avenue, P.O. Box 189, Nashville, TN 37202-0189
8. *The Word Among Us*, P.O. Box 2427, Gaithersburg, MD 20879

BIBLIOGRAPHIES A–C

A

Stress and Illness

1. Benson, Herbert. *The Relaxation Response*. New York: William Morrow and Co., 1975.
2. Elliot, Robert S. *Stress and the Major Cardiovascular Disorders*. New York: Futura Publishing Company, 1979.
3. Friedman, M. and D. Ulmer. *Treating Type A Behavior and Your Heart*. New York: Alfred Knopf, 1984.
4. Rosenman R. H., R. J. Brandt, C. D. Jenkins, M. Friedman, R. Straus, and M. Wurm. "Coronary Heart Disease in the Western Collaborative Group Study: Final Follow-up Experience of 8 1/2 Years." *Journal of the American Medical Assoc.* 233 (1975): 872.
5. Selye, H. *Stress in Health and Disease*. Boston: Butterworth, Inc., 1976.

B
Inner Healing

1. Banks, John B. *Healing Everywhere*. Elizabeth, NJ: St. Luke's Press, 1961.
2. Blackburn, H. H. *God Wants You to Be Well*. Wilton, CT: Morehouse-Barlow Co., 1970.
3. Donnelly, Doris. *Learning to Forgive*. New York: Macmillan Publishing Co., Inc., 1979.
4. Kelsey, Norton. *Healing and Christianity*. San Francisco: Harper and Row, 1973.
5. Kornely, Benno G. *Prayer Service for the Healing of Memories*. Chicago: Loyola University Press, 1981.
6. Krieger, Dolores. *The Therapeutic Touch*. New York: Simon and Schuster, 1979.
7. Linn, Matthew and Dennis Linn. *Healing Life's Hurts: Healing Memories through Five Stages of Forgiveness*. Mahwah, NJ: Paulist Press, 1978.
8. MacNutt, Francis. *The Power to Heal*. Notre Dame, IN: Ave Maria Press, 1977.
9. Maloney, George A. *Broken but Loved*. New York: Alba House, 1981.
10. May, Gerald G. *Care of Mind, Care of Spirit*. San Francisco: Harper and Row, 1982.
11. Nouwen, Henri. *The Wounded Healer*. Garden City, NY: Doubleday, 1972.
12. Reed, William Standish. *Healing the Whole Man*. Old Tappan, NJ: Fleming H. Revell Co., 1969.
13. Sanford, Agnes. *The Healing Gifts of the Spirit*. Philadelphia: A. J. Holman Co., 1966.
14. Sanford, Agnes. *The Healing Light*. Plainfield, NJ: Logos International, 1972.
15. Schickel, Richard. *Singled Out*. New York: Viking Press, 1981.
16. Schlemon, Barbara L. *Healing Prayer*. Notre Dame, IN: Ave Maria Press, 1976.
17. Siegle, Bernie. *Love, Medicine, and Miracles*. New York: Harper and Row, 1987.

18. Simonton, O. C., S. Matthews-Simonton, and J. Creighton. *Getting Well Again*. New York: St. Martin's Press, 1978.
19. Tournier, Paul. *The Adventure of Living*. 1st ed. New York: Harper and Row, 1965.
20. Tournier, Paul. *Reflection*. Philadelphia: Westminster Press, 1976.
21. Tournier, Paul. *The Healing Spirit*. Westchester, IL: Good News Publishers, 1979.
22. Womble-Rufus, J. *Wilt Thou Be Made Whole?* Little Rock, AR: Democrat and Lithographing Co., 1974.
23. Yancy, Philip. *Where Is God When It Hurts?* Wheaton, IL: Campus Life Books, 1977.

C
Prayer and Spirituality

1. Bennett, Dennis J. *Nine O'Clock in the Morning*. Plainfield, NJ: Logos, 1970.
2. Boase, Leonard. *The Prayer of Faith*. Chicago: Loyola University Press, 1985.
3. Bodo, Murray, O.F.M. *The Way of St. Francis*. Garden City, NY: Image Books, 1985.
4. Buechner, Frederick. *The Sacred Journey*. New York: Harper and Row, 1982.
5. Carretto, Carlo. *Letters from the Desert*. Maryknoll, NY: Orbis Books, 1964.
6. Colson, Charles. *Born Again*. Lincoln, VA: Chosen Books, 1976.
7. Day, Albert E. *Discipline and Discovery*. Nashville, TN: The Parthenon Press, 1961.
8. Del Bene, Ron. *The Breath of Life*. Minneapolis: Winston Press, 1981.
9. Del Bene, Ron. *The Hunger of the Heart*. Minneapolis: Winston Press, 1983.
10. Del Bene, Ron. *Alone with God*. Minneapolis: Winston Press, 1984.
11. Diefenbach, Gabriel. *Common Mystic Prayer*. Boston: St. Paul Editions, 1978.
12. de Sales, St. Francis. *Introduction to the Devout Life*. John K. Ryan, trans. and ed. Garden City, NY: Image Books, 1972.
13. Foster, Richard. *Celebration of Discipline*. San Francisco: Harper and Row, 1978.
14. Fraile, Peter A. *God Within Us: Movements, Powers and Joys*. Chicago: Loyola University Press, 1986.
15. Hassel, David J. *Dark Intimacy: Hope for Those in Difficult Prayer Experiences*. Chicago: Loyola University Press, 1986.
16. Higgins, John J. *Thomas Merton on Prayer*. Garden City, NY: Image Books, 1975.

17. Johnston, William. *The Book of Privy Counseling*. Garden City, NY: Image Books, 1973.
18. Johnston, William. *The Cloud of Unknowing*. Garden City, NY: Image Books, 1973.
19. Johnston, William. *Silent Music*. San Francisco: Harper and Row, 1976.
20. Johnston, William. *Christian Zen*. San Francisco: Harper and Row, 1979.
21. Keller, Phillip. *A Shepherd Looks at Psalm 23*. Grand Rapids, MI: Zondervan Publishing House, 1970.
22. Kinnaird, William M. *Joy Comes in the Morning*. Waco, TX: Word Books, 1979.
23. Lawrence, Brother. *The Practice of the Presence of God*. trans. John J. Delaney. Garden City, NY: Image Books, 1958.
24. Lewis, C. S. *The Joyful Christian*. New York: Macmillan Publishing Co., Inc., 1977.
25. Maloney, George. *Prayer of the Heart*. Notre Dame, IN: Ave Maria Press, 1981.
26. Maloney, George. *Called to Intimacy*. Notre Dame, IN: Alba House, 1983.
27. Maloney, George. *Journey into Contemplation*. Locust Valley, NY: Living Flame Press, 1983.
28. Maloney, George. *The Jesus Prayer for Modern Pilgrims*. Everett, WA: Performance Press, 1988.
29. Marshall, Catherine. *The Helper*. Waco, TX: Word Books, 1979.
30. Merton, Thomas. *What Is Contemplation?* Springfield, IL: Templegate Publishers, 1950.
31. Merton, Thomas. *No Man Is An Island*. New York and London: Harcourt Brace Jovanovich, 1955.
32. Morneau, Robert. *Discovering God's Presence*. Collegeville, MN: Liturgical Press, 1978.
33. Morneau, Robert. *Our Father, Revisited*. Collegeville, MN: Liturgical Press, 1978.
34. Murphy, Miriam. *Prayer in Action*. Nashville, TN: Abingdon, 1979.
35. Nee, Watchman. *The Release of the Spirit*. Cloverdale, IN: Sure Foundation Publishers, Ministry of Life, 1965.

36. Paxson, Ruth. *Rivers of Living Water*. Chicago: Moody Press, 1930.
37. Pennington, M. Basil. *Centering Prayer*. Garden City, NY: Image Books, 1982.
38. Sherrill, John. *They Speak with Other Tongues*. Old Tappan, NJ: Revell Press, 1964.
39. Slosser, Bob. *Miracle of Darien*. Plainfield, NJ: Logos International, 1979.
40. Swindel, Charles R. *Growing Strong in the Seasons of Life*. Portland, OR: Multnomah Press, 1983.
41. Teresa, Mother, of Calcutta. *The Love of Christ: Spiritual Counsels*. Georges Gorée and Jean Barbier, eds. San Francisco: Harper and Row, 1982.
42. Webb, Lance. *Disciplines for Life in the Age of Aquarius*. Waco, TX: Word Books, 1972.
43. Webb, Lance. *God's Surprises*. Nashville, TN: Abingdon, 1976.
44. Wilkerson, David. *The Cross and the Switchblade*. New York: Random House, 1963.